Potluck

Publications International, Ltd.

Louis Weber, CEO
Publications International, Ltd.
7373 North Cicero Avenue
Lincolnwood, IL 60712

Pictured on the front cover *(clockwise from top right):* French Carrot Quiche *(page 48),* Strawberry Salad *(page 32),* Sweet and Spicy Sausage Rounds *(page 14)* and Roasted Balsamic Asparagus *(page 60).*
Pictured on the back cover*:* Creamy Chicken Florentine *(page 90).*

ISBN-13: 978-1-4508-2160-5
ISBN-10: 1-4508-2160-X

Library of Congress Control Number: 2011921599

Manufactured in China.

8 7 6 5 4 3 2 1

Microwave Cooking: Microwave ovens vary in wattage. Use the cooking times as guidelines and check for doneness before adding more time.

Preparation/Cooking Times: Preparation times are based on the approximate amount of time required to assemble the recipe before cooking, baking, chilling or serving. These times include preparation steps such as measuring, chopping and mixing. The fact that some preparations and cooking can be done simultaneously is taken into account. Preparation of optional ingredients and serving suggestions is not included.

Publications International, Ltd.

Contents

Apps to Go

Mexi-Meatball Kabobs

Nonstick cooking spray
3 pounds lean ground beef
2 cups quick oats
1 can (12 fluid ounces) NESTLÉ® CARNATION® Evaporated Milk
2 large eggs
½ cup ketchup
2 packets (1¼ ounces *each*) taco seasoning mix
1 teaspoon ground black pepper
3 large bell peppers (any color), cut into 60 (1-inch) pieces
60 (4-inch) wooden skewers
Salsa and sour cream (optional)

PREHEAT oven to 350°F. Foil-line 3 baking sheets and spray with nonstick cooking spray.

COMBINE ground beef, oats, evaporated milk, eggs, ketchup, taco seasoning and black pepper in large bowl until just mixed. Form mixture into 120 (1-inch) meatballs. Place on prepared baking sheets.

BAKE for 15 to 20 minutes or until no longer pink in center. Drain on paper towels, if needed.

THREAD two meatballs and one piece of pepper on *each* skewer. Place on large serving platter. Serve with salsa and sour cream.

Makes 30 servings

Tip: Meatballs can be made and baked ahead of time, refrigerated for up to 3 days or frozen up to 3 months and heated prior to serving.

Tip: Meatballs can also be served individually with toothpicks and dipping bowls of salsas.

Prep Time: 35 minutes • Cook Time: 15 minutes

Asparagus & Prosciutto Antipasto

12 asparagus spears (about 8 ounces)
2 ounces cream cheese, softened
¼ cup (1 ounce) crumbled blue cheese or goat cheese
¼ teaspoon black pepper
1 package (3 to 4 ounces) thinly sliced prosciutto

1. Trim and discard tough ends of asparagus spears. Simmer asparagus in salted water in large skillet 4 to 5 minutes or until crisp-tender. Drain; rinse with cold water until cool. Drain; pat dry with paper towels.

2. Combine cream cheese, blue cheese and pepper in small bowl; mix well. Cut prosciutto slices in half crosswise to make 12 pieces. Spread cream cheese mixture evenly over one side of each prosciutto slice.

3. Wrap each asparagus spear with prosciutto slice. Serve at room temperature or slightly chilled. *Makes 12 appetizers*

Queso-Style Bean Dip

1 can (10¾ ounces) CAMPBELL'S® Condensed Cheddar Cheese Soup
1 cup PACE® Thick & Chunky Salsa
2 tablespoons chopped fresh cilantro leaves or parsley
3 medium green onions, thinly sliced (about ⅓ cup)
1 can (about 15 ounces) black beans, rinsed and drained
Assorted PEPPERIDGE FARM® crackers

1. Mix the soup, salsa, cilantro, green onions and beans in a 1½-quart casserole. Bake at 350°F. for 20 minutes or until hot.

2. Serve with the crackers for dipping. *Makes 4 cups*

Kitchen Tip: Serve this dip in a hollowed out bread round. Simply spoon the baked dip into the bread bowl, then cut up the bread pieces you removed from the loaf and serve with the dip.

Prep Time: 10 minutes • Cook Time: 20 minutes • Total Time: 30 minutes

Asparagus & Prosciutto Antipasto

Cheese & Bacon Jalapeño Rellenos

4 ounces (½ of 8-ounce package) PHILADELPHIA® Cream Cheese, softened
1 cup KRAFT® Shredded Cheddar Cheese
4 slices OSCAR MAYER® Bacon, cooked, crumbled
2 tablespoons finely chopped onions
2 tablespoons chopped cilantro
1 clove garlic, minced
18 jalapeño peppers, cut lengthwise in half, seeds and membranes removed

1. HEAT oven to 375°F. Mix all ingredients except peppers until well blended.

2. SPOON into peppers. Place, filled-sides up, on baking sheet.

3. BAKE 10 minutes or until cheese is melted. *Makes 18 servings*

Substitution: Substitute 3 large red, yellow or green bell peppers, each cut into 6 triangles, for the jalapeño pepper halves. Top with cheese mixture before baking as directed.

Special Extra: Add ¼ teaspoon ground red pepper (cayenne) to the cream cheese mixture before spooning into peppers.

Substitution: Prepare using KRAFT® Shredded Monterey Jack Cheese.

How to Handle Fresh Chile Peppers: When handling fresh chile peppers, be sure to wear disposable rubber or clear plastic gloves to avoid irritating your skin. Never touch your eyes, nose or mouth when handling the peppers. If you've forgotten to wear the gloves and feel a burning sensation in your hands, apply a baking soda and water paste to the affected area. After rinsing the paste off, you should feel some relief.

Prep Time: 20 minutes • Total Time: 30 minutes

Hot & Sweet Deviled Eggs

6 hard-cooked eggs, peeled and cut in half lengthwise
4 to 5 tablespoons mayonnaise
¼ teaspoon curry powder
¼ teaspoon black pepper
⅛ teaspoon salt
Dash of paprika
¼ cup dried sweetened cherries or cranberries, finely chopped
1 teaspoon minced fresh chives
Additional minced fresh chives (optional)

1. Scoop egg yolks into bowl; reserve whites. Mash yolks with mayonnaise until blended. Stir in curry powder, pepper, salt and paprika; mix well. Stir in cherries and 1 teaspoon chives.

2. Pipe or spoon yolk mixture into egg whites. Garnish with additional chives. *Makes 12 servings*

Ultimate Nachos

1 pound ground beef
¾ cup water
1 package (1.12 ounces) taco seasoning mix
1 can (15.6 ounces) refried beans
5 cups tortilla chips
2 cups PACE® Chunky Salsa
1 cup shredded Cheddar cheese (about 4 ounces)
⅓ cup sliced jalapeño pepper

1. Cook the beef in a 10-inch skillet over medium-high heat until it's well browned, stirring to break up meat. Pour off any fat.

2. Stir in the water and taco seasoning. Heat to a boil. Reduce the heat to low. Cook for 5 minutes, stirring occasionally.

3. Heat the beans according to the package directions.

4. Place the chips on a large platter. Layer the beef mixture, beans, salsa, cheese and pepper over the chips. *Makes 8 servings*

Prep Time: 5 minutes • **Cook Time:** 20 minutes • **Total Time:** 25 minutes

Hot & Sweet Deviled Eggs

Thai-Peanut Ginger Wings

- 1 can (12 fluid ounces) NESTLÉ® CARNATION® Evaporated Milk
- 1 cup creamy or chunky peanut butter
- ½ cup soy sauce, *divided*
- ¼ cup chopped green onions
- 2½ teaspoons ground ginger
- 2 teaspoons rice or cider vinegar
- ½ teaspoon red pepper flakes
- 5 pounds frozen chicken wings, thawed

PLACE evaporated milk, peanut butter, *3 tablespoons* soy sauce, green onions, ginger, vinegar and pepper flakes in blender; cover. Blend until smooth. Combine ½ cup peanut sauce, *remaining 5 tablespoons* soy sauce and chicken wings in large bowl; cover. Marinate chicken in refrigerator for 1 hour. Refrigerate remaining peanut sauce.

PREHEAT oven to 425°F. Foil-line and grease 2 baking sheets with sides.

PLACE chicken on prepared baking sheets. Discard any remaining marinade.

BAKE for 40 to 45 minutes, turning once, or until chicken is cooked through. Remove from baking sheets to serving platter. Stir remaining peanut sauce and spoon some over wings. If desired, serve remaining sauce with wings and assorted cut up vegetables. *20 servings*

Tip: Jazz up the presentation with a colorful array of fresh vegetables, such as peapods and red and yellow peppers.

Prep Time: 15 minutes • **Marinate Time:** 1 hour • **Cook Time:** 40 minutes

Sweet and Spicy Sausage Rounds

1 pound kielbasa sausage, sliced
⅔ cup blackberry jam
⅓ cup steak sauce
1 tablespoon yellow mustard
½ teaspoon ground allspice

Slow Cooker Directions

1. Place all ingredients in slow cooker; toss to coat completely. Cover; cook on HIGH 3 hours or until glazed.

2. Serve with decorative cocktail picks. *Makes about 16 servings*

The Famous Lipton® California Dip

1 envelope LIPTON® RECIPE SECRETS® Onion Soup Mix
1 container (16 ounces) sour cream

Blend LIPTON® RECIPE SECRETS® Onion Soup Mix with sour cream in small bowl; chill at least 2 hours. Serve with your favorite dippers.
Makes about 2 cups dip

Tip: For a creamier dip, add more sour cream.

Sensational Spinach Dip: Add 1 package (10 ounces) frozen chopped spinach, thawed and squeezed dry.

California Seafood Dip: Add 1 cup finely chopped cooked clams, crabmeat or shrimp, ¼ cup chili sauce and 1 tablespoon horseradish.

California Bacon Dip: Add ⅓ cup crumbled cooked bacon or bacon bits.

California Blue Cheese Dip: Add ¼ pound crumbled blue cheese and ¼ cup finely chopped walnuts.

Mini Dizzy Dogs

½ sheet refrigerated crescent roll dough (half of 8-ounce can)
20 mini hot dogs or smoked sausages
Ketchup and mustard

1. Preheat oven to 375°F. Line baking sheet with parchment paper.

2. Cut dough lengthwise into 20 (¼-inch) strips. Wrap 1 dough strip around each hot dog. Place on prepared baking sheet.

3. Bake 10 to 12 minutes or until light golden brown. Serve with ketchup and mustard for dipping. *Makes 20 appetizers*

Roasted Garlic Hummus

2 tablespoons Roasted Garlic (recipe follows)
1 can (about 15 ounces) chickpeas, rinsed and drained
¼ cup fresh parsley sprigs
2 tablespoons water
2 tablespoons lemon juice
½ teaspoon curry powder
⅛ teaspoon dark sesame oil
Dash hot pepper sauce (optional)
Pita bread wedges and fresh vegetables

1. Prepare Roasted Garlic.

2. Place chickpeas, parsley, 2 tablespoons Roasted Garlic, water, lemon juice, curry powder, sesame oil and hot pepper sauce, if desired, in food processor or blender. Cover; process until smooth.

3. Serve with pita wedges and vegetables. *Makes 6 servings*

Roasted Garlic: Preheat oven to 400°F. Remove outer layers of papery skin and cut ¼ inch off top of garlic head. Place cut side up on a piece of heavy-duty foil. Drizzle with 2 teaspoons olive oil; wrap tightly in foil. Bake 25 to 30 minutes or until cloves feel soft when pressed. Cool slightly before squeezing out garlic pulp.

Olive Tapenade

1 can (16 ounces) medium pitted black olives
½ cup pimiento-stuffed green olives
1 tablespoon roasted garlic*
½ teaspoon dry mustard
½ cup (2 ounces) crumbled feta cheese
1 tablespoon olive oil
Toast slices

**To roast garlic, preheat oven to 400°F. Remove outer layers of papery skin and cut ¼ inch off top of garlic head. Place cut side up on a piece of heavy-duty foil. Drizzle with 2 teaspoons olive oil; wrap tightly in foil. Bake 25 to 30 minutes or until cloves feel soft when pressed. Cool slightly before squeezing out garlic pulp.*

1. Process olives, roasted garlic and mustard in food processor or blender until finely chopped.

2. Combine olive mixture, cheese and oil in medium bowl; stir until well blended. Serve with toast slices. *Makes 1¾ cups tapenade*

Tip: For the best flavor, prepare this tapenade several hours or one day ahead to allow the flavors to blend and refrigerate until serving.

Spinach, Artichoke and Feta Dip

½ cup thawed frozen chopped spinach
1 cup crumbled feta cheese
½ teaspoon black pepper
1 cup marinated artichokes, undrained
Toasted bread or crackers

1. Place spinach in small microwavable bowl; microwave on HIGH 1 minute.

2. Place cheese and pepper in food processor. Process 1 minute or until finely chopped. Add artichokes and spinach; process 30 seconds until well mixed but not puréed. Serve with toasted bread.

Makes about 1½ cups

Greek-Style Chicken Wings with Tzatziki Sauce

Tzatziki Sauce (recipe follows)
2 tablespoons olive oil, divided
5 pounds chicken wings, tips removed and split at joints
2 teaspoons dried oregano
½ teaspoon salt
¼ teaspoon black pepper
2 tablespoons fresh lemon juice

Slow Cooker Directions

1. Prepare Tzatziki Sauce.

2. Heat 1 tablespoon oil in large nonstick skillet over medium-high heat. Brown chicken wings in batches about 3 minutes on each side. Transfer to slow cooker.

3. Sprinkle with oregano. Drizzle with remaining 1 tablespoon oil and toss gently to coat. Cover; cook on HIGH 3 to 3½ hours or until tender. Season with salt, pepper and lemon juice. Toss gently to coat. Serve with Tzatziki sauce. *Makes 8 servings*

Tzatziki Sauce

1 medium cucumber
2 cups Greek-style strained yogurt
2 tablespoons fresh lemon juice
2 tablespoons olive oil
1 clove garlic, crushed
½ teaspoon salt

1. Peel cucumber. Slice in half lengthwise. Scoop seeds from both halves of cucumber and discard. Coarsely grate cucumber into medium bowl.

2. Stir in yogurt, lemon juice, oil and garlic. Season with salt. Cover and refrigerate until serving. *Makes about 2¼ cups*

Cheesy Quichettes

12 slices bacon, crisp-cooked and crumbled
6 eggs
¼ cup whole milk
1½ cups refrigerated shredded hash brown potatoes
¼ cup chopped fresh parsley
½ teaspoon salt
1½ cups (6 ounces) shredded Mexican cheese blend

1. Preheat oven to 400°F. Lightly spray 12 standard (2½-inch) muffin cups with nonstick cooking spray.

2. Place equal amounts of bacon into prepared muffin cups. Beat eggs and milk in medium bowl. Add potatoes, parsley and salt; mix well. Spoon mixture evenly into muffin cups.

3. Bake 15 minutes or until knife inserted into centers comes out almost clean. Sprinkle with cheese; let stand 3 minutes or until cheese melts. (Egg mixture will continue to cook while standing.*) To remove from pan, gently run knife around outer edges and lift out with fork. *Makes 12 quichettes*

**Standing also allows for easier removal of quichettes from pan.*

Layered Mexican Dip

1 package (8 ounces) cream cheese, softened
1 tablespoon plus 1 teaspoon taco seasoning mix
1 cup canned black beans
1 cup salsa
1 cup shredded lettuce
1 cup (4 ounces) shredded Cheddar cheese
½ cup chopped green onions
2 tablespoons sliced pitted ripe olives
Tortilla chips

1. Combine cream cheese and seasoning mix in small bowl. Spread on bottom of 9-inch pie plate.

2. Layer black beans, salsa, lettuce, cheese, green onions and olives over cream cheese mixture. Refrigerate until ready to serve. Serve with tortilla chips. *Makes 10 servings*

Prep Time: 10 minutes

Barbecue Bacon Party Spread

2 packages (8 ounces each) PHILADELPHIA® Cream Cheese, softened
½ cup KRAFT THICK 'N SPICY® Original Barbecue Sauce
1 package (2.8 ounces) OSCAR MAYER® Real Bacon Recipe Pieces
1 small tomato, chopped
½ cup chopped green bell pepper
⅓ cup sliced green onions
1½ cups KRAFT® Shredded Cheddar Cheese
TRISCUIT® Thin Crisps

1. SPREAD cream cheese on large platter; drizzle with barbecue sauce.

2. TOP with all remaining ingredients except the Thin Crisps.

3. SERVE with the Thin Crisps. *Makes 35 servings*

Prep Time: 15 minutes

Mexican Pizza

½ of a 17.3-ounce package PEPPERIDGE FARM® Puff Pastry Sheets (1 sheet), thawed
¾ cup PREGO® Traditional Italian Sauce
¼ cup PACE® Picante Sauce
¾ cup shredded mozzarella cheese
¾ cup shredded Cheddar cheese
¼ cup sliced pitted ripe olives

1. Heat the oven to 400°F.

2. Unfold the pastry sheet on a lightly floured surface. Roll the pastry sheet into a 15×10-inch rectangle. Place the pastry onto a baking sheet. Prick the pastry thoroughly with a fork. Bake for 10 minutes or until the pastry is golden brown.

3. Stir the Italian sauce and picante sauce in a small bowl. Spread the sauce mixture on the pastry to within ½ inch of the edges. Top with the cheeses and sprinkle with the olives. Bake for 5 minutes or until the cheeses are melted. *Makes 4 servings*

Thaw Time: 40 minutes • Prep Time: 20 minutes • Bake Time: 15 minutes

Barbecue Bacon Party Spread

Salads & Such

German Potato Salad

10 medium potatoes
1¾ cups SWANSON® Beef Broth (Regular, Lower Sodium or Certified Organic)
¼ cup cider vinegar
¼ cup all-purpose flour
3 tablespoons sugar
½ teaspoon celery seed
⅛ teaspoon ground black pepper
1 medium onion, chopped (about ½ cup)
3 tablespoons chopped fresh parsley

1. Place the potatoes into a 4-quart saucepan. Add water to cover. Heat over high heat to a boil. Reduce the heat to low. Cook for 20 minutes or until the potatoes are tender. Drain. Let cool and cut in cubes. Place the potatoes into a large bowl.

2. Stir the broth, vinegar, flour, sugar, celery seed and black pepper in the saucepan. Stir in the onion. Cook and stir over medium-high heat until the mixture boils and thickens. Reduce the heat to low. Cook for 5 minutes or until the onion is tender.

3. Add the parsley and broth mixture to the potatoes and stir to coat. Serve warm. *Makes 12 servings*

Kitchen Tip: You can let this dish stand for a few minutes before serving. The dressing will soak into the warm potatoes—delicious!

Prep Time: 15 minutes • Cook Time: 30 minutes • Total Time: 45 minutes

Pasta and Grilled Vegetable Salad with Cilantro Dressing

DRESSING

1 can (4 ounces) ORTEGA® Fire-Roasted Diced Green Chiles
¼ cup chopped fresh cilantro
¼ cup olive oil
1 tablespoon REGINA® Red Wine Vinegar
½ teaspoon POLANER® Minced Garlic
Salt and black pepper, to taste

SALAD

1 red bell pepper, cored, seeded, cut in half
1 green bell pepper, cored, seeded, cut in half
1 medium zucchini, cut lengthwise into thin slices
1 medium yellow squash, cut lengthwise into thin slices
1 large red onion, cut into ½-inch-thick wedges
1 pound pasta shells or penne, cooked
1 jar (16 ounces) ORTEGA® Garden Vegetable Salsa
¼ cup firmly packed fresh basil, cut into thin strips
Lettuce leaves (optional)

COMBINE chiles, cilantro, oil, vinegar and garlic in small bowl. Whisk until well blended. Season with salt and pepper to taste. Set aside.

PREHEAT grill to medium-high heat, about 15 minutes. Lightly brush grill grid with vegetable oil.

GRILL bell peppers, zucchini, squash and onion 3 to 5 minutes per side or until fork-tender. Remove vegetables from grill; cut into bite-size pieces.

TOSS cooked pasta, salsa, sliced vegetables and basil in large bowl or on serving platter. Serve with dressing on lettuce leaves, if desired.

Makes 6 to 8 servings

Prep Time: 15 minutes • Start to Finish Time: 30 minutes

Salami, Wild Rice and Whole Wheat Rotini Salad

2½ cups water
½ teaspoon salt, divided
⅔ cup uncooked wild rice
1½ cups cooked whole wheat rotini
1 cup grape tomatoes, halved lengthwise
4 ounces hard salami, cut into ¼-inch dice
1 large stalk celery, finely chopped
1 large roasted red pepper, diced
¼ cup finely chopped green onions
2 tablespoons olive oil
2 teaspoons white wine vinegar
1 teaspoon Dijon mustard
⅛ teaspoon black pepper

1. Combine water and ¼ teaspoon salt in medium saucepan. Bring to a boil. Stir in wild rice. Cover; reduce heat to low. Cook 45 minutes or until tender. Drain well and cool.

2. Combine rice, rotini, tomatoes, salami, celery, red pepper and green onions in large bowl. Combine oil, vinegar, mustard, black pepper and remaining ¼ teaspoon salt in small bowl. Stir to mix well. Pour over salad. Toss gently to mix well. *Makes 4 servings*

Tip: To roast a fresh red bell pepper, place it on a stovetop over an open flame or 4 inches from the heat in a broiler. Turn frequently to blacken all sides using long-handled tongs. Place the blackened pepper in a paper or plastic bag, shut the bag and set it aside for 30 minutes to loosen the skin. Scrape off the blackened skin with a paring knife.

Salami, Wild Rice and Whole Wheat Rotini Salad

Strawberry Salad

2 packages (4-serving size each) strawberry gelatin
1 cup boiling water
2 packages (10 ounces each) frozen strawberries, thawed
1 can (20 ounces) crushed pineapple, drained
2 cups sour cream
Whipped topping and sliced fresh strawberries

Combine gelatin and water in large bowl; stir until dissolved. Add strawberries and pineapple; mix well. Pour half of gelatin mixture into large bowl. Refrigerate until soft set. Spread sour cream over gelatin in pan. Pour remaining gelatin mixture over sour cream. Refrigerate until ready to serve. Top with whipped topping and fresh strawberries.

Makes 12 to 14 servings

Grilled Peach Salad with Spinach and Red Onion Vinaigrette

3 tablespoons plus 1 teaspoon extra virgin olive oil, divided
2 tablespoons rice wine vinegar *or* 1½ tablespoons balsamic vinegar
2 tablespoons finely chopped red onion
1 tablespoon chopped fresh tarragon or basil, *or* 1 teaspoon dried tarragon or basil, crushed
Salt and black pepper
1 cup DOLE® Frozen Sliced Peaches, partially thawed
1 package (9 ounces) DOLE® Spinach or Spring Mix Salad Blends
½ cup crumbled feta or goat cheese

WHISK 3 tablespoons olive oil and vinegar in small bowl. Add onion, tarragon, salt and pepper.

BRUSH peach slices with remaining 1 teaspoon olive oil. Grill over a medium-hot fire or on a stovetop grill pan over medium heat until lightly browned, about 4 to 5 minutes. Cool for 1 minute.

COMBINE spinach, peaches and cheese in large bowl. Add vinaigrette; gently toss to coat.

Makes 4 servings

Prep Time: 20 minutes • Grill Time: 5 minutes

Strawberry Salad

Nine-Layer Salad

6 cups baby spinach, packed
1½ cups grape tomatoes
2 cups pattypan squash, blanched and halved crosswise
1 cup peas, blanched
4 ounces baby corn, halved lengthwise
2 cups baby carrots, blanched and halved lengthwise
1 cup peppercorn-ranch salad dressing
1 cup shredded Cheddar cheese
4 slices bacon, crisp-cooked and crumbled

1. Layer spinach, tomatoes, squash, peas, corn and carrots in 4-quart glass bowl. Pour dressing over salad; spread evenly. Top with cheese. Cover and refrigerate 4 hours.

2. Before serving, sprinkle with bacon. *Makes 7 servings*

Belgioioso® Fresh Mozzarella Ciliegine and Grape Tomato Appetizer

12 ounces BELGIOIOSO® Fresh Mozzarella Ciliegine
1 pint grape tomatoes
¾ cup Italian vinaigrette
16 small wooden skewers
Freshly ground black pepper and salt

Drain the liquid from the BELGIOIOSO® Fresh Mozzarella Ciliegine, reserving some for storing any leftover cheese. Place the ciliegine in a large bowl. Rinse grape tomatoes well and remove any stems. Drain well and add to bowl with cheese. Add vinaigrette to bowl and toss gently with cheese and tomatoes.

Alternate grape tomatoes and ciliegine on skewers. Top with black pepper and salt, then serve. *Makes 8 servings*

Mexican Slaw

1 (6-inch) corn tortilla, cut into thin strips
Nonstick cooking spray
¼ teaspoon chili powder
3 cups shredded green cabbage
1 cup shredded red cabbage
½ cup shredded carrots
½ cup sliced radishes
½ cup corn
¼ cup coarsely chopped fresh cilantro
¼ cup mayonnaise
1 tablespoon fresh lime juice
2 teaspoons cider vinegar
1 teaspoon honey
½ teaspoon ground cumin
¼ teaspoon salt
¼ teaspoon black pepper

1. Preheat oven to 350°F. Arrange tortilla strips in even layer on nonstick baking sheet. Spray strips with cooking spray and sprinkle with chili powder. Bake 6 to 8 minutes or until crisp.

2. Combine cabbage, carrots, radishes, corn and cilantro in large bowl. Combine mayonnaise, lime juice, vinegar, honey, cumin, salt and pepper in small bowl. Add mayonnaise mixture to cabbage mixture; toss gently to coat. Top with baked tortilla strips. *Makes 8 servings*

Zesty Zucchini Chickpea Salad

- 3 medium zucchini
- ½ teaspoon salt
- 5 tablespoons white vinegar
- 1 clove garlic, minced
- ¼ teaspoon dried thyme
- ½ cup olive oil
- 1 cup canned chickpeas, rinsed and drained
- ½ cup sliced pitted black olives
- 3 green onions, minced
- 1 canned chipotle pepper in adobo sauce, drained, seeded and minced
- 1 ripe avocado
- ⅓ cup crumbled feta *or* 3 tablespoons grated Romano cheese
- Boston lettuce leaves
- Sliced tomato and fresh cilantro sprigs (optional)

1. Cut zucchini lengthwise into halves; cut halves crosswise into ¼-inch-thick slices. Place slices in medium bowl; sprinkle with salt. Toss to mix. Spread zucchini on several layers of paper towels. Let stand at room temperature 30 minutes to drain.

2. Combine vinegar, garlic and thyme in large bowl. Gradually whisk in oil until dressing is thoroughly blended. Pat zucchini dry; add to dressing. Add chickpeas, olives and green onions; toss lightly to coat. Cover; refrigerate at least 30 minutes or up to 4 hours, stirring occasionally.

3. Stir in chipotle pepper just before serving. Peel, pit and cut avocado into ½-inch cubes. Add avocado and cheese to salad; toss lightly to mix. Serve salad in lettuce-lined bowl. Garnish with tomato and cilantro, if desired.

Makes 4 to 6 servings

Layered Taco Salad

Nonstick cooking spray
½ pound ground beef
1½ teaspoons chili powder
1½ teaspoons ground cumin, divided
½ cup picante sauce
1 teaspoon sugar
6 cups shredded romaine lettuce
2 plum tomatoes, seeded and diced
½ cup chopped green onions
¼ cup chopped fresh cilantro
28 nacho-flavored tortilla chips, crumbled
½ cup sour cream
½ cup (2 ounces) shredded sharp Cheddar or Mexican blend cheese

1. Spray medium nonstick skillet with cooking spray; heat over medium-high heat. Brown beef 3 to 5 minutes, stirring to break up meat. Drain fat. Stir in chili powder and 1 teaspoon cumin. Let cool.

2. Combine picante sauce, sugar and remaining ½ teaspoon cumin in small bowl.

3. Place lettuce in 11×7-inch serving dish. Layer with beef, tomatoes, green onions, cilantro and chips. Top with sour cream; sprinkle with cheese. Spoon picante sauce mixture on top. *Makes 4 to 6 servings*

Pesto Rice Salad

2 cups MINUTE® White Rice, uncooked
1 package (7 ounces) basil pesto sauce
1 cup cherry tomatoes, halved
8 ounces whole-milk mozzarella cheese, cut into ½-inch cubes
⅓ cup Parmesan cheese, shredded
Toasted pine nuts (optional)

Prepare rice according to package directions. Place in large bowl. Let stand 10 minutes.

Add pesto sauce; mix well. Gently stir in tomatoes and cheeses.

Serve warm or cover and refrigerate until ready to serve. Sprinkle with pine nuts, if desired. *Makes 6 servings*

Tip: To toast pine nuts, spread in single layer in heavy-bottomed skillet. Cook over medium heat 1 to 2 minutes, stirring frequently, until nuts are lightly browned. Remove from skillet immediately. Cool before using.

Tip: For a heartier meal, add 1 package (6 ounces) grilled chicken breast strips to the prepared salad.

Fiesta Pasta Salad

12 ounces tricolor rotini pasta
1 cup ORTEGA® Garden Vegetable Salsa
¼ cup mayonnaise
1 cup frozen whole-kernel corn, thawed
1 cup ORTEGA® Black Beans, drained
2 tablespoons ORTEGA® Diced Jalapeños
3 green onions, diced
½ cup chopped fresh cilantro

Cook pasta according to package directions. Cool.

Combine pasta, salsa, mayonnaise, corn, beans, jalapeños, green onions and cilantro in large bowl; mix well. Refrigerate at least 30 minutes before serving. *Makes 6 to 8 servings*

Tip: For an elegant first course or brunch item, serve this salad in stemmed wine or martini glasses, in lettuce cups made from Bibb or iceberg lettuce.

Prep Time: 5 minutes • **Start to Finish:** 45 minutes

Pesto Rice Salad

Take-and-Shake Salad

1 can (about 15 ounces) chickpeas, rinsed and drained
1 pint grape tomatoes, halved
1 can (14 ounces) quartered artichoke hearts, drained
4 ounces crumbled feta cheese *or* 1 cup cooked diced chicken breast
4 ounces sliced mushrooms
1 can (2¼ ounces) sliced ripe olives, drained
½ medium green bell pepper, chopped
⅔ cup cider vinegar
1½ tablespoons extra virgin olive oil
2 teaspoons sugar
1 teaspoon dried oregano
¼ teaspoon black pepper
5 cups chopped romaine lettuce

1. Combine chickpeas, tomatoes, artichoke hearts, cheese, mushrooms, olives and bell pepper in large bowl; toss gently to blend. Place in large food storage container.

2. Combine vinegar, oil, sugar, oregano and black pepper in small bowl; whisk until blended. Pour dressing into small food storage container.

3. Place lettuce in jumbo food storage bag.

4. When ready to serve, add chickpea mixture to lettuce. Pour in salad dressing and shake to combine. Transfer to serving bowl.

Makes 5 servings

Sweet Italian Marinated Vegetable Salad

½ can (14 ounces) quartered artichoke hearts, drained
5 ounces grape or cherry tomatoes, halved
½ cup chopped green bell pepper
¼ cup finely chopped red onion
2 ounces mozzarella cheese, cut into ¼-inch cubes
2 tablespoons white or rice wine vinegar
1 tablespoon chopped fresh oregano *or* 1 teaspoon dried oregano
2 teaspoons sugar
⅛ teaspoon salt
⅛ teaspoon red pepper flakes

Combine all ingredients in medium bowl; toss to coat. Serve immediately or refrigerate 1 hour to allow flavors to blend. *Makes 4 servings*

Sweet Potato & Fruit Salad

2 sweet potatoes, cooked, peeled and diced
1 Granny Smith apple, unpeeled and chopped
¼ cup chopped celery
1 container (6 ounces) plain yogurt
2 tablespoons orange juice
½ to 1 teaspoon grated fresh ginger
½ teaspoon curry powder
⅛ teaspoon salt
½ cup cinnamon-coated nuts, divided
¼ cup drained mandarin oranges

1. Combine sweet potatoes, apple and celery in large bowl.

2. Combine yogurt, orange juice, ginger, curry powder and salt in small bowl. Add to sweet potato mixture; toss to coat. Add half of nuts; stir gently. Top with remaining nuts and oranges. Refrigerate until ready to serve.
Makes 4 to 6 servings

Sweet Italian Marinated Vegetable Salad

Muffuletta Rice Salad

SALAD
- 1 package HILLSHIRE FARM® Smoked Sausage
- 4 cups cooked long grain white rice, cooled
- 1 cup provolone or mozzarella cheese cubes
- ¾ cup chopped celery
- ½ cup coarsely chopped pimiento-stuffed green olives
- ½ cup sliced ripe olives
- ⅓ cup chopped sweet onion
- ⅓ cup chopped fresh basil

DRESSING
- ½ cup olive oil
- ⅓ cup balsamic or red wine vinegar
- 1 tablespoon minced garlic
- 2 teaspoons dried oregano
- 1 teaspoon ground black pepper
- ¾ teaspoon sugar

1. Cut sausage into ½ inch cubes. Heat a large nonstick skillet on medium-high for 3 minutes. Add sausage and cook, stirring frequently, for 3 to 4 minutes or until lightly browned.

2. Combine sausage with all salad ingredients in large bowl.

3. Whisk dressing ingredients together in small bowl until thoroughly combined. Pour over salad, tossing lightly to combine. Cover and refrigerate for at least 4 hours or up to 24 hours before serving.

Makes 10 servings

Sides to Share

French Carrot Quiche

1 pound carrots
1 tablespoon butter, plus additional for greasing dishes
¼ cup chopped green onions
½ teaspoon herbes de Province
1 cup milk
¼ cup whipping cream
½ cup flour
2 eggs, lightly beaten
½ teaspoon minced fresh thyme
¼ teaspoon ground nutmeg
½ cup shredded Gruyère or Swiss cheese

1. Peel carrots and cut into rounds. Butter four shallow 1-cup baking dishes or one 9-inch quiche dish or shallow casserole. Preheat oven to 350°F.

2. Melt 1 tablespoon butter in large skillet over medium heat. Cook and stir carrots, green onions and herbes de Provence 3 to 4 minutes or until carrots are tender.

3. Meanwhile, combine milk and cream in medium bowl; whisk in flour gradually. Stir in eggs, thyme and nutmeg.

4. Spread carrot mixture in prepared dishes; add milk mixture. Sprinkle with cheese. Bake 20 to 25 minutes for individual quiches or 30 to 40 minutes for 9-inch quiche or until firm. Serve warm or at room temperature. *Makes 4 servings.*

Mexican Cowboy Beans

3 strips bacon, diced
1 onion, diced
½ teaspoon POLANER® Chopped Garlic
2 cans (15 ounces each) pinto or light red kidney beans
1 can (4 ounces) ORTEGA® Fire-Roasted Diced Green Chiles
½ cup ORTEGA® Original Salsa, Medium
½ teaspoon ground cumin

Brown bacon in large skillet over medium-high heat 4 minutes, stirring occasionally to prevent sticking. Add onion and garlic; cook until onion is browned, about 4 minutes more. Stir in beans, chiles, salsa and cumin. Reduce heat to low. Simmer 15 minutes or until slightly thickened.

Makes 6 to 8 servings

Note: For a complete meal, stir these beans into cooked rice and serve over ORTEGA® Soft Flour Tortillas topped with grated cheese.

Prep Time: 5 minutes • Start to Finish: 25 minutes

Ziti Ratatouille

1 large eggplant, peeled and cut into ½-inch cubes (about 1½ pounds)
2 medium zucchini, sliced
1 green or red bell pepper, cut into ½-inch pieces
1 onion, chopped
4 cloves garlic, minced
1 jar (about 24 ounces) marinara sauce
2 cans (about 14 ounces each) diced tomatoes with garlic and onions
8 ounces uncooked ziti pasta
1 can (6 ounces) pitted black olives, drained
Lemon juice
Parmesan cheese

Slow Cooker Directions

1. Layer eggplant, zucchini, bell pepper, onion, garlic, marinara sauce and tomatoes in slow cooker. Cover and cook on LOW 4½ hours.

2. Stir in pasta and olives. Cover; cook 25 minutes or until pasta is tender. Drizzle with lemon juice and sprinkle with cheese. *Makes 6 to 8 servings*

Mexican Cowboy Beans

Cheesy Corn and Peppers

2 pounds frozen corn
2 poblano peppers, chopped
2 tablespoons butter, cubed
1 teaspoon salt
½ teaspoon ground cumin
¼ teaspoon black pepper
1 cup (4 ounces) shredded sharp Cheddar cheese
1 package (3 ounces) cream cheese, cubed

Slow Cooker Directions

1. Coat slow cooker with nonstick cooking spray. Add corn, poblanos, butter, salt, cumin and black pepper. Cover; cook on HIGH 2 hours.

2. Add Cheddar cheese and cream cheese; stir to blend. Cover; cook 15 minutes or until cheeses are melted. *Makes 8 servings*

Prep Time: 8 minutes • **Cook Time:** 2¼ hours

Mexican Corn Bread Pudding

1 can (14¾ ounces) cream-style corn
¾ cup yellow cornmeal
1 can (4 ounces) diced mild green chiles
2 eggs
2 tablespoons sugar
2 tablespoons vegetable oil
2 teaspoons baking powder
¾ teaspoon salt
½ cup shredded Cheddar cheese

Slow Cooker Directions

Coat 2-quart slow cooker with nonstick cooking spray. Combine corn, cornmeal, chiles, eggs, sugar, oil, baking powder and salt in medium bowl. Stir well to blend. Pour into slow cooker. Cover; cook on LOW 2 to 2½ hours or until center is set. Sprinkle cheese over top. Cover and let stand 5 minutes or until cheese is melted. *Makes 8 servings*

Cheesy Corn and Peppers

Scalloped Potatoes with Ham

2 tablespoons unsalted butter
1 tablespoon all-purpose flour
¾ teaspoon salt
¼ teaspoon black pepper
1¼ cups whipping cream
1¼ cups whole milk
2 cups shredded Swiss cheese, divided
1½ pounds russet potatoes
1 medium onion, cut into thin rings and separated
½ pound sliced or cubed baked ham

1. Preheat oven to 350°F. Grease 12×8-inch baking dish.

2. Melt butter in medium saucepan over medium heat; whisk in flour, salt and pepper. Cook 1 minute. Gradually whisk in cream and milk. Bring to a boil; remove from heat. Stir in 1½ cups cheese in two or three batches. Set aside.

3. Peel potatoes. Cut into ⅛-inch-thick slices. Layer one third of potato slices, half of onion slices and one third of potato slices in prepared dish. Cover with half of white sauce. Layer with remaining half of onion slices, ham and one third of potato slices. Top with remaining half of white sauce.

4. Cover with foil; bake 50 to 55 minutes or until potatoes are almost tender. Sprinkle with remaining ½ cup cheese. Bake 10 to 15 minutes or until cheese is golden. Let stand 10 minutes before serving.

Makes about 6 servings

Greek Rice Bake

1 can (10¾ ounces) CAMPBELL'S® Condensed Cream of Mushroom Soup (Regular or 98% Fat Free)
½ cup water
1 can (about 14.5 ounces) diced tomatoes, undrained
1 jar (6 ounces) marinated artichoke hearts, drained and cut in half
2 portobello mushrooms, coarsely chopped (about 2 cups)
¾ cup uncooked quick-cooking brown rice
1 can (about 15 ounces) small white beans, rinsed and drained
3 to 4 tablespoons crumbled feta cheese

1. Heat the oven to 400°F. Stir the soup, water, tomatoes, artichokes, mushrooms, rice and beans in a 2-quart casserole. Cover the casserole.

2. Bake for 40 minutes or until the rice is tender. Stir the rice mixture. Let stand for 5 minutes. Sprinkle with the cheese before serving.

Makes 6 servings

Kitchen Tip: Different brands of quick-cooking brown rice cook differently, so the bake time for this recipe may be slightly longer or shorter than indicated.

Prep Time: 15 minutes • Cook Time: 45 minutes • Total Time: 1 hour

Beans with Smoky Canadian Bacon

2 cans (about 14 ounces each) diced fire-roasted tomatoes
1 can (about 15 ounces) pinto beans, rinsed and drained
1 package (8 ounces) Canadian bacon, cut into ½-inch cubes
½ cup Texas-style barbecue sauce*
1 onion, finely chopped
½ teaspoon salt
Black pepper
⅛ teaspoon crushed red pepper flakes (optional)

**Look for barbecue sauce with liquid smoke as an ingredient.*

Slow Cooker Directions

Combine all ingredients in slow cooker. Cover; cook on LOW 5 to 7 hours.

Makes 4 servings

Prep Time: 10 minutes • Cook Time: 5 to 7 hours

Greek Rice Bake

Eggplant Tomato Gratin

Vegetable cooking spray
1 large eggplant (about 1¼ pounds) cut into ½-inch thick slices
1 can (10¾ ounces) CAMPBELL'S® Condensed Cream of Celery Soup (Regular or 98% Fat Free)
½ cup milk
¼ cup grated Parmesan cheese
2 large tomatoes, cut into ½-inch thick slices (about 2 cups)
1 medium onion, thinly sliced (about ½ cup)
¼ cup chopped fresh basil leaves
¼ cup Italian-seasoned dry bread crumbs
1 tablespoon chopped fresh parsley (optional)
1 tablespoon olive oil

1. Heat the oven to 425°F. Spray a baking sheet with cooking spray. Arrange the eggplant in a single layer. Bake for 20 minutes or until tender, turning halfway through baking. Spray 3-quart shallow baking dish with cooking spray.

2. Stir the soup, milk and cheese in a small bowl.

3. Layer **half** the eggplant, tomatoes, onion, basil and soup mixture in the prepared dish. Repeat the layers.

4. Stir the bread crumbs, parsley, if desired, and oil in a small bowl. Sprinkle over the soup mixture.

5. Reduce the heat to 400°F. and bake for 25 minutes or until hot and golden brown. Let stand for 10 minutes. *Makes 8 servings*

Kitchen Tip: Can be prepared ahead up to topping with the bread crumb mixture. Cover and refrigerate overnight. Add the bread crumb mixture and bake at 400°F. for 30 minutes or until hot and golden brown.

Prep Time: 20 minutes • **Bake Time:** 45 minutes • **Stand Time:** 10 minutes

Roasted Balsamic Asparagus

1 pound fresh asparagus
1 tablespoon olive oil
½ teaspoon salt
¼ teaspoon black pepper
1 tablespoon balsamic glaze*
¼ cup finely shredded or grated Parmesan cheese

**Look for balsamic glaze in the condiment section of the supermarket.*

Preheat oven to 375°F. Place asparagus in shallow 11×7-inch baking dish. Drizzle oil over asparagus. Use tongs to roll asparagus to coat evenly with oil; sprinkle with salt and pepper. Bake 14 to 16 minutes or until crisp-tender. Drizzle balsamic glaze over asparagus; roll again with tongs to coat. Top with cheese. *Makes 6 servings*

Swiss Vegetable Casserole

1 can (10¾ ounces) CAMPBELL'S® Condensed Cream of Mushroom Soup (Regular or 98% Fat Free)
⅓ cup sour cream
¼ teaspoon ground black pepper
1 bag (16 ounces) frozen vegetable combination (broccoli, cauliflower, carrots), thawed
1 can (2.8 ounces) French fried onions (1⅓ cups), divided
½ cup shredded Swiss cheese

1. Stir soup, sour cream, black pepper, vegetables, ⅔ cup onions and ¼ cup cheese in 2-quart casserole. Cover casserole.

2. Bake at 350°F. for 40 minutes or until the vegetables are tender. Stir the vegetable mixture. Top with the remaining onions and cheese.

3. Bake for 5 minutes or until the cheese is melted. *Makes 4 servings*

For Cheddar Cheese Lovers: Use Cheddar cheese instead of Swiss cheese.

Kitchen Tip: If you like, stir 1 jar (4 ounces) chopped pimientos, drained, into the vegetable mixture before baking.

Prep Time: 5 minutes • **Bake Time:** 45 minutes • **Total Time:** 50 minutes

Roasted Balsamic Asparagus

Heavenly Sweet Potatoes

Vegetable cooking spray
1 can (40 ounces) cut sweet potatoes in heavy syrup, drained
¼ teaspoon ground cinnamon
⅛ teaspoon ground ginger
¾ cup SWANSON® Chicken Broth (Regular, Natural Goodness® or Certified Organic)
2 cups miniature marshmallows

1. Heat the oven to 350°F.

2. Spray a 1½-quart casserole with cooking spray.

3. Put the potatoes, cinnamon and ginger in an electric mixer bowl. Beat at medium speed until almost smooth. Add the broth and beat until potatoes are fluffy. Spoon the potato mixture in the prepared dish. Top with the marshmallows.

4. Bake for 20 minutes or until heated through and marshmallows are golden brown.

Makes 8 servings

Cheddar-Swiss Strata

6 cups cubed French bread or Italian bread
1 can (10¾ ounces) CAMPBELL'S® Condensed Cheddar Cheese Soup
1 cup milk
4 eggs
1½ cups shredded Swiss cheese (about 6 ounces)

1. Place the bread cubes into a greased 2-quart shallow baking dish. Beat the soup, milk, eggs and cheese in a medium bowl with a fork or whisk. Pour the soup mixture over the bread cubes. Stir and press the bread cubes into the milk mixture to coat. Cover and refrigerate overnight.

2. Bake, uncovered, at 350°F. for 40 minutes or until a knife inserted in the center comes out clean.

Makes 6 servings

Tip: This recipe may be doubled. Divide the ingredients between 2 greased 2-quart shallow baking dishes. Bake as directed above.

Heavenly Sweet Potatoes

Mexican Corn Pudding

6 ORTEGA® Yellow Corn Taco Shells
1 can (14 ounces) creamed corn
1 cup canned or frozen corn, drained
1 cup milk
2 eggs
1 can (4 ounces) ORTEGA® Diced Green Chiles
¼ cup ORTEGA® Taco Sauce, any variety
¼ cup (½ stick) butter, melted
½ cup (2 ounces) shredded Cheddar cheese

PREHEAT oven to 350°F.

PLACE taco shells in food processor and pulse until evenly ground. Place in medium bowl. Add creamed corn, corn, milk, eggs, chiles, taco sauce and butter; blend well. Pour into 9-inch pie pan. Sprinkle evenly with cheese.

BAKE 50 minutes. Allow to cool slightly before serving. *Makes 8 servings*

TIP: To crush taco shells without a food processor, place them in a resealable plastic food storage bag and run a rolling pin over the shells until they're evenly crushed.

Prep Time: 5 minutes • Start to Finish: 55 minutes

Tangy Pineapple Sweet Potato Casserole

4 medium sweet potatoes, peeled and cut into ¼-inch slices (about 4 cups)
1 can (20 ounces) DOLE® Pineapple Slices, drained *or* 2 cups DOLE® Frozen Tropical Gold Pineapple Chunks, partially thawed
½ cup dried cranberries or DOLE® Seedless Raisins
½ cup packed brown sugar
3 tablespoons butter or margarine, melted
½ teaspoon ground cinnamon

PREHEAT oven to 400°F. Spray 12×8-inch baking dish with nonstick cooking spray.

ARRANGE sweet potatoes, pineapple and cranberries in baking dish. Sprinkle with brown sugar. Combine butter and cinnamon in small bowl; drizzle over brown sugar. Cover with aluminum foil.

BAKE 45 to 50 minutes or until potatoes are tender. Remove aluminum foil last 5 to 10 minutes of baking time. *Makes 6 servings*

Not Your Gramma's Kugel

Vegetable cooking spray
1 package (12 ounces) uncooked medium egg noodles (about 7 cups)
½ cup currants
1 can (10¾ ounces) CAMPBELL'S® Condensed Cheddar Cheese Soup
1 cup cottage cheese
¾ cup sugar
1 teaspoon grated orange zest
2 eggs

Slow Cooker Directions

1. Spray the inside of a 3½-quart slow cooker with the cooking spray. Cook the noodles according to the package directions until they're almost tender. Drain and place them in the cooker. Sprinkle with the currants.

2. Beat the soup, cottage cheese, sugar, orange zest and eggs in a medium bowl with a fork. Pour over the noodles and stir to coat.

3. Cover and cook on LOW for 2 to 2½ hours or until it's set. Serve warm. *Makes 6 servings*

Tangy Pineapple Sweet Potato Casserole

Scalloped Tomatoes & Corn

1 can (15 ounces) cream-style corn
1 can (about 14 ounces) diced tomatoes
¾ cup saltine cracker crumbs
1 egg, lightly beaten
2 teaspoons sugar
¾ teaspoon black pepper
Chopped fresh tomatoes (optional)
Chopped fresh Italian parsley (optional)

Slow Cooker Directions

1. Combine corn, diced tomatoes, cracker crumbs, egg, sugar and pepper in slow cooker; mix well.

2. Cover; cook on LOW 4 to 6 hours. Sprinkle with fresh tomatoes and parsley before serving, if desired. *Makes 4 to 6 servings*

Prep Time: 7 minutes • **Cook Time:** 4 to 6 hours

Chorizo and Corn Dressing

½ pound chorizo sausage, casings removed
1 can (about 14 ounces) reduced-sodium chicken broth
1 can (10¾ ounces) condensed cream of chicken soup, undiluted
1 box (6 ounces) corn bread stuffing mix
1 cup chopped onion
1 cup diced red bell pepper
1 cup chopped celery
1 cup frozen corn
3 eggs, lightly beaten

Slow Cooker Directions

1. Lightly coat inside of slow cooker with nonstick cooking spray.

2. Cook chorizo in large skillet over medium-high heat until browned, stirring to break up meat. Transfer to slow cooker with slotted spoon and return skillet to heat.

3. Whisk broth and soup into drippings in skillet. Add stuffing mix, onion, bell pepper, celery, corn and eggs; stir until well blended. Stir into slow cooker. Cover; cook on LOW 7 hours or on HIGH 3½ hours.

Makes 4 to 6 servings

Scalloped Tomatoes & Corn

Slow Cooker Spinach Risotto

2 teaspoons butter
2 teaspoons olive oil
3 tablespoons finely chopped shallot
1¼ cups uncooked arborio rice
½ cup dry white wine
3 cups chicken broth
2 cups baby spinach
¼ cup grated Parmesan cheese
2 tablespoons pine nuts, toasted

Slow Cooker Directions

1. Heat butter and oil in medium skillet over medium heat until butter is melted. Add shallot; cook and stir 1 minute or until softened.

2. Stir in rice; cook 2 minutes or until well coated. Stir in wine and cook until reduced by half. Transfer to slow cooker. Stir in broth.

3. Cover; cook on HIGH 2 to 2½ hours or until rice is almost tender but some liquid remains in slow cooker. Stir in spinach. Cover; cook 15 to 20 minutes or until spinach is wilted and rice is tender and creamy. Stir in Parmesan cheese and pine nuts just before serving. *Makes 4 servings*

Main Events

Classic Chili

1½ pounds ground beef
1½ cups chopped onion
1 cup chopped green bell pepper
2 cloves garlic, minced
3 cans (about 15 ounces each) dark red kidney beans, rinsed and drained
2 cans (about 15 ounces each) tomato sauce
1 can (about 14 ounces) diced tomatoes
2 to 3 teaspoons chili powder
1 to 2 teaspoons dry hot mustard
¾ teaspoon dried basil
½ teaspoon black pepper
1 to 2 dried hot chile peppers (optional)

Slow Cooker Directions

1. Cook beef, onion, bell pepper and garlic in large skillet 6 to 8 minutes or until meat is browned and onion is tender. Drain fat. Transfer beef mixture to 5-quart slow cooker.

2. Add beans, tomato sauce, tomatoes, chili powder, mustard, basil, black pepper and chile peppers, if desired; mix well. Cover; cook on LOW 8 to 10 hours or on HIGH 4 to 5 hours.

3. Remove chile peppers before serving.

Makes 6 servings

California Picnic Loaf

- 1 (7- to 8-inch) round loaf sourdough bread
- ½ cup shredded Colby-Monterey Jack cheese
- ¼ cup salsa
- ¼ cup mayonnaise
- 1 cup shredded romaine lettuce
- 2 cups cooked chicken breast, chopped
- ¼ cup sliced pitted black olives
- 1 avocado, thinly sliced

1. Slice off top one third of bread, creating a lid; set aside. Scoop out soft bread insides, leaving a hollow shell.*

2. Combine cheese, salsa and mayonnaise in small bowl. Spread half on bottom of bread shell. Top with lettuce. Layer with chicken, remaining salsa mixture, olives and avocado. Press down for a firm filling. Cover with top lid of bread.

3. Wrap in plastic or foil and refrigerate up to 4 hours for easier slicing. When ready to serve, cut into 4 to 6 wedges. *Makes 4 to 6 servings*

**Use leftover bread to make homemade croutons. Cut or tear into bite-size pieces, toss with a small amount of olive oil and dried herbs, spread onto a baking sheet and bake at 350°F for 10 to 12 minutes or until browned.*

Sausage Pizza Pie Casserole

8 ounces mild Italian sausage, casings removed
1 package (about 14 ounces) refrigerated pizza dough
½ cup tomato sauce
2 tablespoons chopped fresh basil *or* 2 teaspoons dried basil
½ teaspoon dried oregano
¼ teaspoon red pepper flakes
3 ounces mushrooms, quartered
½ cup thinly sliced red onion
½ cup thinly sliced green bell pepper
½ cup seeded diced tomato
½ cup sliced pitted black olives
8 slices smoked provolone cheese
2 tablespoons grated Parmesan and Romano cheese blend

1. Preheat oven to 350°F. Lightly coat 13×9-inch baking dish with nonstick cooking spray.

2. Brown sausage in large nonstick skillet over medium-high heat 6 to 8 minutes, stirring to break up meat. Drain fat.

3. Line prepared baking dish with pizza dough. Spoon sauce evenly over dough; sprinkle with basil, oregano and red pepper flakes. Layer with sausage, mushrooms, onion, bell pepper, tomato, olives and provolone cheese. Roll sides of crust to form rim.

4. Bake 20 to 25 minutes or until bottom and sides of crust are golden brown. Sprinkle with cheese blend; let stand 5 minutes before serving.

Makes 4 to 6 servings

Sausage Pizza Pie Casserole

Chicken Cassoulet

- 4 slices bacon
- ¼ cup all-purpose flour
- Salt and black pepper
- 1¾ pounds bone-in chicken pieces
- 2 cooked chicken sausages, cut into ¼-inch pieces
- 1 medium onion, chopped
- 1½ cups diced red and green bell peppers
- 2 cloves garlic, minced
- 1 teaspoon dried thyme
- 1 teaspoon olive oil
- 2 cans (about 15 ounces each) cannellini or Great Northern beans, rinsed and drained
- ½ cup dry white wine

1. Preheat oven to 350°F. Cook bacon in large skillet over medium-high heat until crisp; drain on paper towels. Cut into 1-inch pieces.

2. Pour off all but 2 tablespoons fat from skillet. Place flour in shallow bowl; season with salt and black pepper. Dip chicken pieces into flour mixture; shake off excess. Brown chicken in batches over medium-high heat; remove to plate. Lightly brown sausages; remove to plate.

3. Add onion, bell peppers, garlic and thyme to skillet. Cook and stir over medium heat 5 minutes or until softened, adding oil as needed to prevent sticking. Transfer onion mixture to 13×9-inch baking dish. Add beans; mix well. Top with chicken, sausages and bacon. Add wine to skillet; cook and stir over medium heat, scraping up browned bits. Pour over casserole.

4. Cover; bake 40 minutes. Uncover; bake 15 minutes or until chicken is cooked through (165°F).

Makes 6 servings

Meat Loaf Cupcakes

3 medium potatoes, peeled and chopped
1½ pounds ground beef
½ cup finely chopped onion
⅓ cup old-fashioned oats
1 egg
2 tablespoons chopped fresh rosemary leaves
½ cup milk
2 tablespoons butter
1 teaspoon salt
Black pepper
¼ cup snipped fresh chives

1. Preheat oven to 350°F. Place potatoes in medium saucepan; cover with water. Bring to a boil; cook 25 to 30 minutes or until fork-tender.

2. Meanwhile, combine beef, onion, oats, egg and rosemary in large bowl; mix well. Divide mixture among 10 standard (2½-inch) muffin cups or silicone baking cups. Bake 25 minutes or until cooked through (160°F).

3. Beat potatoes, milk, butter, salt and pepper in large bowl with electric mixer at medium speed 3 minutes or until smooth. Place mashed potato mixture in large piping bag fitted with large star tip.

4. Remove meat loaf cupcakes to serving platter. Pipe mashed potatoes on top for frosting. Sprinkle with chives.

Makes 10 servings

Cheesy Chicken Enchiladas

¼ cup (½ stick) butter
1 cup chopped onion
2 cloves garlic, minced
¼ cup all-purpose flour
1 cup chicken broth
4 ounces cream cheese, softened and cut into pieces
2 cups (8 ounces) shredded Mexican cheese blend, divided
1 cup shredded cooked chicken
1 can (7 ounces) diced mild green chiles, drained
½ cup diced pimientos
6 (8-inch) flour tortillas, warmed
¼ cup chopped fresh cilantro
¾ cup salsa

1. Preheat oven to 350°F. Spray 13×9-inch baking dish with nonstick cooking spray.

2. Melt butter in medium saucepan over medium heat. Add onion and garlic; cook and stir until onion is tender. Add flour; cook and stir 1 minute. Gradually add chicken broth; cook and stir 2 to 3 minutes or until slightly thickened. Add cream cheese; stir until melted. Stir in ½ cup shredded cheese, chicken, chiles and pimientos.

3. Spoon about ⅓ cup mixture onto each tortilla. Roll up and place seam side down in prepared dish. Pour remaining mixture over enchiladas; sprinkle with remaining 1½ cups shredded cheese.

4. Bake 20 minutes or until bubbly and lightly browned. Sprinkle with cilantro and serve with salsa. *Makes 6 servings*

Mexican Tossed Layer Casserole

1 cup uncooked rice
¾ pound ground beef
¾ cup picante sauce
1 teaspoon ground cumin
2 cups (8 ounces) shredded sharp Cheddar cheese, divided
½ cup sour cream
⅓ cup finely chopped green onions
2 tablespoons chopped fresh cilantro
½ teaspoon salt
⅛ teaspoon ground red pepper

1. Cook rice according to package directions. Preheat oven to 350°F. Lightly coat 11×7-inch baking dish with nonstick cooking spray.

2. Brown beef in large nonstick skillet over medium-high heat 6 to 8 minutes, stirring to break up meat. Drain fat. Add picante sauce and cumin; stir well.

3. Stir 1 cup cheese, sour cream, green onions, cilantro, salt and red pepper into rice. Spoon rice mixture into prepared baking dish. Top with beef mixture.

4. Cover with foil; bake 20 minutes or until heated through. Sprinkle with remaining 1 cup cheese. Bake, uncovered, 3 minutes or until cheese is melted.

Makes 4 servings

Stuffed Party Baguette

2 medium red bell peppers
1 loaf French bread (about 14 inches long)
¼ cup plus 2 tablespoons Italian dressing, divided
1 small red onion, very thinly sliced
8 large fresh basil leaves
3 ounces Swiss cheese, very thinly sliced

1. Preheat oven to 425°F. Cover baking sheet with foil.

2. To roast bell peppers, cut in half; remove stems, seeds and membranes. Place peppers, cut sides down, on prepared baking sheet. Bake 20 to 25 minutes or until skins are blackened.

3. Transfer peppers to paper bag; close bag. Let stand 10 minutes or until peppers are cool enough to handle and skins are loosened. Peel off and discard skins; cut peppers into strips.

4. Trim ends from bread. Cut loaf in half lengthwise. Remove soft insides of loaf and reserve for another use.

5. Brush ¼ cup dressing evenly onto cut sides of bread. Arrange pepper strips on bottom half of loaf; top with onion. Brush onion with remaining 2 tablespoons dressing; top with basil and cheese. Replace bread top. Wrap loaf tightly in plastic wrap; refrigerate at least 2 hours.

6. Cut loaf crosswise into 1-inch slices. Secure with toothpicks.

Makes 12 servings

Baked Chicken & Broccoli

1 pound broccoli, trimmed, cut into 1-inch pieces, cooked and drained
8 skinless, boneless chicken breasts
1 can (26 ounces) CAMPBELL'S® Condensed Cream of Mushroom Soup (Regular or 98% Fat Free)
⅔ cup milk
¼ teaspoon ground black pepper
8 cups hot cooked rice

1. Place broccoli and chicken in 3-quart shallow baking dish. Mix soup, milk and pepper and pour over all.

2. Bake at 400°F. for 30 minutes or until done. Stir sauce before serving. Serve with the rice.
Makes 8 servings

Kitchen Tip: Substitute 1 bag (16 ounces) frozen broccoli cuts, thawed and drained for fresh. To thaw broccoli, microwave on HIGH 5 minutes.

Prep Time: 15 minutes • **Cook Time:** 30 minutes • **Total Time:** 45 minutes

Chicken Zucchini Casserole

1 package (about 6 ounces) herb stuffing mix
½ cup (1 stick) butter, melted
2 cups cubed zucchini, blanched and drained
1 can (14 ounces) condensed cream of celery soup, undiluted
1½ cups chopped cooked chicken
1 cup grated carrots
½ cup sour cream
1 small onion, chopped
½ cup (2 ounces) shredded Cheddar cheese

1. Preheat oven to 350°F.

2. Combine stuffing mix and butter in medium bowl; reserve 1 cup of mixture. Place remaining stuffing in 13×9-inch baking dish.

3. Combine zucchini, soup, chicken, carrots, sour cream and onion in large bowl. Pour mixture over stuffing in baking dish. Top with remaining 1 cup stuffing mixture and cheese. Bake 40 to 45 minutes or until heated through and cheese is melted.
Makes 8 servings

Baked Chicken & Broccoli

Taco Casserole

- 1 pound lean ground beef
- ½ cup chopped onion
- 1 bottle (8 ounces) ORTEGA® Taco Sauce
- ¾ cup water
- 1 can (4 ounces) ORTEGA® Fire-Roasted Diced Green Chiles
- 1 packet (1.25 ounces) ORTEGA® 40% Less Sodium Taco Seasoning Mix
- 1 package (12-count) ORTEGA® Whole Grain Corn Taco Shells, broken, divided
- 2 cups (8 ounces) shredded Cheddar cheese, divided
- Toppings: chopped tomatoes, chopped green bell pepper, sour cream

PREHEAT oven to 375°F. Grease 11×7-inch baking dish.

COOK beef and onion in large skillet over medium heat, stirring occasionally, until beef is browned. Drain and discard excess fat.

STIR in taco sauce, water, chiles and seasoning mix; bring to a boil. Reduce heat to low. Cook 3 to 4 minutes, stirring occasionally.

LAYER half of broken taco shells on bottom of prepared baking dish. Cover with half of meat mixture; sprinkle with 1 cup cheese. Repeat layers with remaining ingredients.

BAKE 20 to 25 minutes or until bubbly and cheese is melted. Serve with desired toppings.

Makes 8 servings

Prep Time: 10 minutes • **Start to Finish:** 30 minutes

Creamy Chicken Florentine

- 1 can (10¾ ounces) CAMPBELL'S® Condensed Cream of Chicken Soup (Regular or 98% Fat Free)
- 1½ cups water
- ½ of a 20-ounce bag frozen cut leaf spinach, thawed and well drained (about 3½ cups)
- 1 can (about 14.5 ounces) Italian-style diced tomatoes
- 1 pound skinless, boneless chicken breasts, cut into 1-inch cubes
- 2½ cups uncooked penne pasta
- ½ cup shredded mozzarella cheese

1. Heat the oven to 375°F. Stir the soup, water, spinach, tomatoes and chicken in a 3-quart shallow baking dish. Cover the baking dish.

2. Bake for 20 minutes. Cook the pasta according to the package directions and drain well in a colander. Uncover the baking dish and stir in the pasta.

3. Bake for 20 minutes or until the pasta mixture is hot and bubbling. Sprinkle with the cheese. Let stand for 5 minutes or until the cheese is melted.

Makes 4 servings

Prep Time: 15 minutes • **Bake Time:** 40 minutes • **Stand Time:** 5 minutes

Layered Pasta Casserole

- 8 ounces uncooked penne pasta
- 8 ounces mild Italian sausage, casings removed
- 8 ounces ground beef
- 1 jar (about 26 ounces) pasta sauce
- 1 package (10 ounces) frozen chopped spinach, thawed and squeezed dry
- 2 cups (8 ounces) shredded mozzarella cheese, divided
- 1 cup ricotta cheese
- ½ cup grated Parmesan cheese
- 1 egg
- 2 tablespoons chopped fresh basil *or* 2 teaspoons dried basil
- 1 teaspoon salt

1. Preheat oven to 350°F. Spray 13×9-inch baking dish with nonstick cooking spray. Cook pasta according to package directions; drain. Transfer to prepared dish.

2. Brown sausage and beef 6 to 8 minutes in large skillet over medium-high heat, stirring to break up meat. Drain fat. Add pasta sauce; mix well. Add half of meat sauce to pasta; toss to coat.

3. Combine spinach, 1 cup mozzarella, ricotta, Parmesan, egg, basil and salt in medium bowl. Spoon small mounds of spinach mixture over pasta mixture; spread evenly with back of spoon. Top with remaining meat sauce; sprinkle with remaining 1 cup mozzarella. Bake 30 minutes or until heated through.

Makes 6 to 8 servings

Layered Pasta Casserole

Key Lime Bars

1½ cups finely crushed graham crackers (10 to 12 crackers)
4 tablespoons packed brown sugar
2 tablespoons all-purpose flour
5 tablespoons melted butter
8 ounces cream cheese, softened
1½ cups granulated sugar
2 eggs
¼ cup freshly squeezed Key lime juice
1 tablespoon grated lime peel
Lime slices

1. Preheat oven to 350°F. Grease 13×9-inch baking pan.

2. For crust, combine graham cracker crumbs, brown sugar and flour in large bowl. Gradually add melted butter, stirring until thoroughly moist and crumbly.

3. Press crust evenly into bottom of pan. Bake 15 minutes.

4. For filling, beat cream cheese and granulated sugar in large bowl with electric mixer at medium-low speed until smooth and creamy. Add eggs, one at a time, beating well after each addition. Add lime juice and lime peel. Mix until just combined.

5. Pour filling over warm crust. Bake in center of oven 15 to 20 minutes or until filling is set and begins to separate from sides of pan.

6. Cool on wire rack 2 hours. Garnish with lime slices. Cut into bars.

Makes 24 bars

Limoncello Cupcakes

Cupcakes
- 1 package (about 18 ounces) lemon cake mix
- 4 eggs
- 1 package (4-serving size) lemon instant pudding and pie filling mix
- ½ cup vegetable oil
- ½ cup vodka
- ½ cup water

Glaze
- 4 cups powdered sugar
- ⅓ cup lemon juice
- 3 to 4 tablespoons vodka
- Candied lemon peel
- Coarse sugar (optional)

1. Preheat oven to 350°F. Line 24 standard (2½-inch) muffin cups with paper baking cups.

2. Beat cake mix, eggs, pudding mix, oil, ½ cup vodka and water in large bowl with electric mixer at low speed until smooth. Spoon batter evenly into prepared muffin cups. Bake 15 minutes or until toothpick inserted into centers comes out clean. Cool completely in pans on wire racks.

3. For glaze, whisk powdered sugar, lemon juice and 3 tablespoons vodka in medium bowl until smooth. Add remaining 1 tablespoon vodka if icing is too stiff. Dip tops of cupcakes in glaze; garnish with candied lemon peel. Sprinkle with coarse sugar, if desired. Let stand until set.

Makes 24 cupcakes

Easy Strawberry Mousse Pie

1 cup boiling water
1 package (4-serving size) strawberry gelatin
2 extra ripe, medium DOLE® Bananas
1 carton (6 ounces) strawberry yogurt
2 cups thawed whipped topping, plus additional for garnish
1 cup DOLE® Frozen Whole or Sliced Strawberries, partially thawed, quartered or sliced, plus additional for garnish
1 (9-inch) prepared pie crust

STIR boiling water into gelatin in medium bowl at least 2 minutes or until completely dissolved. Place in freezer about 20 minutes or until slightly thickened, stirring occasionally.

PLACE bananas in blender or food processor container. Cover; blend until smooth (1 cup).

COMBINE yogurt and puréed bananas in large bowl. Blend gelatin mixture into banana mixture. Refrigerate until slightly thickened. Fold whipped topping into gelatin mixture with strawberries.

SPOON gelatin mixture into prepared crust. Refrigerate 4 hours or until firm. Garnish with additional whipped topping and strawberries, if desired.

Makes 8 servings

Prep Time: 30 minutes • **Chill Time:** 4 hours

Chocolate Pecan Bars

Crust
- 1⅓ cups all-purpose flour
- ½ cup (1 stick) unsalted butter, softened
- ¼ cup packed brown sugar
- ½ teaspoon salt

Topping
- ¾ cup light corn syrup
- 3 eggs, lightly beaten
- 2 tablespoons unsalted butter, melted and cooled
- ½ teaspoon vanilla
- ½ teaspoon almond extract
- ¾ cup milk chocolate chips
- ¾ cup semisweet chocolate chips
- ¾ cup chopped pecans, toasted*
- ¾ cup granulated sugar

**To toast pecans, spread in single layer in heavy-bottomed skillet. Cook over medium heat 1 to 2 minutes, stirring frequently, until nuts are lightly browned. Remove from skillet immediately. Cool before using.*

1. Preheat oven to 350°F. Coat 13×9-inch baking pan with nonstick cooking spray.

2. For crust, combine flour, ½ cup butter, brown sugar and salt in medium bowl with fork until mixture is crumbly. Press evenly into prepared baking pan. Bake 12 to 15 minutes or until light brown. Let stand 10 minutes.

3. Meanwhile, for topping, combine corn syrup, eggs, 2 tablespoons butter, vanilla and almond extract in large bowl; stir with fork until combined (do not beat). Fold in chocolate chips, pecans and granulated sugar until blended. Pour over warm crust.

4. Bake 25 to 30 minutes or until toothpick inserted into center comes out clean. Cool completely on wire rack before cutting into squares. Refrigerate in airtight container. *Makes 24 bars*

Tip: For easy removal of corn syrup, first coat the inside of the measuring cup with nonstick cooking spray.

Chocolate Pecan Bars

Berry Chocolate Cookie Tartlets

1¼ cups (about ⅓ tub) NESTLÉ® TOLL HOUSE® Refrigerated Sugar Cookie Tub Dough, slightly softened
⅓ cup plus 1 tablespoon all-purpose flour
½ cup NESTLÉ® TOLL HOUSE® Semi-Sweet Chocolate Morsels
½ cup dried cranberries or cherries, chopped

PREHEAT oven to 325°F.

COMBINE cookie dough and flour in large mixing bowl. Divide dough into 24 (1-inch balls). Press dough into mini muffin cups.*

BAKE for 10 minutes or until light golden brown around edges and puffy.

REMOVE tartlets from oven and immediately fill with morsels and cranberries. Cool for 10 minutes in muffin cups. Carefully remove to wire rack. Do not invert; cool completely. *Makes 2 dozen tartlets*

**If making tartlets in batches, keep extra dough in the refrigerator.*

Brownie Pizza

REYNOLDS® Parchment Paper
1 package (about 19 ounces) fudge brownie mix
1 tub (16 ounces) ready-to-spread frosting, any flavor
Chocolate covered candies, colored sprinkles, mini marshmallows or nuts

Preheat oven to 350°F. Line a large cookie sheet with REYNOLDS Parchment Paper. Trace a 12-inch circle on parchment paper; set aside.

Prepare brownie mix following package directions for fudge brownies. Pour batter in center of parchment paper on cookie sheet; spread batter evenly inside circle.

Bake 20 to 22 minutes or until wooden pick inserted in center comes out clean. Cool on wire rack. Frost brownie pizza, leaving a 1-inch border unfrosted for the pizza "crust." Decorate with candies, sprinkles, marshmallows or nuts. Cut into wedges with a pizza cutter to serve.
Makes 12 servings

Berry Chocolate Cookie Tartlets

Chocolate Mini Cheesecakes

Chocolate Crumb Crust (recipe follows)
½ cup HERSHEY'S® Cocoa
¼ cup (½ stick) butter or margarine, melted
3 packages (8 ounces each) cream cheese, softened
1 can (14 ounces) sweetened condensed milk (not evaporated milk)
3 eggs
2 teaspoons vanilla extract
Chocolate Glaze (recipe follows)

1. Heat oven to 300°F. Line 24 muffin cups (2½ inches in diameter) with paper bake cups or spray with vegetable cooking spray.* Press about 1 tablespoonful Chocolate Crumb Crust mixture onto bottom of each cup.

2. Stir together cocoa and ¼ cup butter. Beat cream cheese until fluffy. Beat in cocoa mixture. Gradually beat in sweetened condensed milk. Beat in eggs and vanilla. Fill muffin cups with batter.

3. Bake 35 minutes or until set. Cool 15 minutes; remove from pan to wire rack. Cool completely. Refrigerate. Before serving, spread with Chocolate Glaze. Allow to set. Serve at room temperature.

Makes 24 mini cheesecakes

**If vegetable cooking spray is used, cool baked cheesecakes. Freeze 15 minutes; remove with narrow spatula.*

Chocolate Crumb Crust: Stir together 1½ cups vanilla wafer crumbs (about 45 wafers, crushed), 6 tablespoons HERSHEY'S® Cocoa, 6 tablespoons powdered sugar and 6 tablespoons melted butter or margarine in medium bowl.

Chocolate Glaze: Melt 1 cup HERSHEY'S® SPECIAL DARK® Chocolate Chips or HERSHEY'S® Semi-Sweet Chocolate Chips with ½ cup whipping cream and ½ teaspoon vanilla extract in medium saucepan over low heat. Stir until smooth. Use immediately. Makes about 1 cup glaze.

Gimme S'more Pie

- 1 can (12 fluid ounces) NESTLÉ® CARNATION® Evaporated Milk, *divided*
- 1 package (3.4 ounces) chocolate instant pudding and pie filling mix
- 1 (6-ounce) *prepared* 9-inch graham cracker crumb crust
- 3 cups mini marshmallows, *divided*
- 2 cups frozen whipped topping, thawed
- ½ cup NESTLÉ® TOLL HOUSE® Milk Chocolate Morsels

WHISK *1¼ cups* evaporated milk and pudding mix in medium bowl until well blended. Pour into crust.

MICROWAVE 2 cups marshmallows and *remaining ¼ cup* evaporated milk in medium, uncovered, microwave-safe bowl on HIGH (100%) power for 30 to 45 seconds; stir until smooth. Let stand for 15 minutes. Gently fold in whipped topping. Spoon marshmallow mixture over chocolate layer; smooth top with spatula.

REFRIGERATE for 2 hours or until set. Top with remaining 1 cup marshmallows and morsels.

Makes 8 servings

Tip: For a gooey s'more topping, place chilled pie on a baking sheet. Preheat broiler. Place baking sheet with pie on rack 6 inches from broiler unit (pie top should be at least 4 inches from broiler unit). Broil for 30 seconds or until marshmallows are light brown and morsels are shiny. Watch carefully as browning occurs very fast! A handheld butane kitchen torch can be used as well.

HERSHEY'®S Brownies with Peanut Butter Frosting

- ½ cup (1 stick) butter or margarine
- 4 sections (½ ounce each) HERSHEY'®S Unsweetened Chocolate Baking Bar, broken into pieces
- 1 cup sugar
- 2 eggs
- 1 teaspoon vanilla extract
- ½ cup all-purpose flour
- ¼ teaspoon baking powder
- ¼ teaspoon salt
- ½ cup chopped nuts
- Peanut Butter Frosting (recipe follows, optional)

1. Heat oven to 350°F. Grease 8-inch square baking pan.

2. Melt butter and chocolate in medium saucepan over low heat. Remove from heat; stir in sugar. Beat in eggs and vanilla with wooden spoon. Stir together flour, baking powder and salt. Add to chocolate mixture, blending well. Stir in nuts. Pour batter into prepared pan.

3. Bake 30 to 35 minutes or until brownies begin to pull away from sides of pan. Cool completely in pan on wire rack. Frost with Peanut Butter Frosting, if desired. Cut into squares. *Makes about 16 brownies*

Peanut Butter Frosting

- 1 cup powdered sugar
- ¼ cup REESE'S® Creamy Peanut Butter
- 2 tablespoons milk
- ½ teaspoon vanilla extract

Combine all ingredients in small bowl; beat until smooth. If necessary, add additional milk, ½ teaspoon at a time, until of desired consistency.
Makes about ¾ cup frosting

HERSHEY'®S Brownies with Peanut Butter Frosting

Peach-Cherry Pie

¾ cup granulated sugar
3 tablespoons instant tapioca
1 teaspoon grated lemon peel
½ teaspoon ground cinnamon
⅛ teaspoon salt
4 cups fresh peach slices (about 7 medium peaches)
2 cups sweet cherries such as Bing, pitted
1 tablespoon lemon juice
½ (about 15 ounce) package refrigerated pie crusts
2 tablespoons unsalted butter, cubed
Streusel Topping (recipe follows)
Vanilla ice cream (optional)

1. Preheat oven to 375°F. Combine granulated sugar, tapioca, lemon peel, cinnamon and salt in large bowl.

2. Add peach slices, cherries and lemon juice to sugar mixture; toss until fruit is well mixed.

3. Line pie pan with crust following package directions. Transfer fruit mixture to crust. Dot with butter.

4. Prepare Streusel Topping; sprinkle over pie filling. Bake 40 to 45 minutes or until juices are bubbly. Serve warm or at room temperature with ice cream, if desired. Refrigerate leftovers. *Makes 8 servings*

Streusel Topping: Combine ¾ cup old-fashioned oats, ⅓ cup all-purpose flour, ⅓ cup packed brown sugar and ¾ teaspoon ground cinnamon in medium bowl. Stir in 4 tablespoons melted unsalted butter until mixture is crumbly.

REESE'S® Marble Cheesecake

Crumb Crust (page 114)
3 packages (8 ounces each) cream cheese, softened
1 cup sugar, divided
½ cup dairy sour cream
1 tablespoon vanilla extract
3 eggs
3 tablespoons all-purpose flour
¼ cup HERSHEY'S® Cocoa
1 tablespoon vegetable oil
1⅓ cups REESE'S® Peanut Butter Chips
¼ cup milk

1. Heat oven to 450°F. Prepare Crumb Crust.

2. Beat cream cheese, ¾ cup sugar, sour cream and vanilla in large bowl on medium speed of electric mixer until smooth. Add eggs and flour; beat until blended.

3. Beat cocoa, remaining ¼ cup sugar and oil with 1½ cups cheese mixture in medium bowl. Place peanut butter chips and milk in small microwave-safe bowl. Microwave at MEDIUM (50%) 30 seconds; stir. If necessary, microwave at MEDIUM an additional 15 seconds at a time, stirring after each heating, until chips are melted when stirred. Gradually add warm peanut butter mixture to remaining vanilla batter; beat on high speed 5 minutes.

4. Spoon peanut butter and chocolate mixtures alternately over prepared crust. Gently swirl with knife or spatula for marbled effect.

5. Bake 10 minutes.* Without opening oven door, decrease temperature to 250°F. and continue to bake 30 minutes. Turn off oven; leave cheesecake in oven 30 minutes without opening door. Remove from oven to wire rack; with knife, loosen cake from side of pan. Cool completely; remove side of pan. Refrigerate until serving time. Cover; refrigerate leftover cheesecake.

Makes 12 servings

**Cheesecakes are less likely to crack if baked in a water bath.*

continued on page 114

REESE'S® Marble Cheesecake, continued

Crumb Crust

⅓ cup REESE'S® Peanut Butter Chips
1¼ cups vanilla wafer crumbs (about 40 wafers, crushed)
¼ cup HERSHEY'S® Cocoa
¼ cup powdered sugar
¼ cup (½ stick) butter or margarine, melted

With knife or food processor, chop peanut butter chips. Stir together crumbs, cocoa, powdered sugar and butter in medium bowl. Stir in chopped peanut butter chips. Press firmly onto bottom of 9-inch springform pan or 9-inch square pan.

Whoopie Pie Cupcakes

1 package (about 18 ounces) dark chocolate cake mix, plus ingredients to prepare mix
½ cup (1 stick) unsalted butter, softened
¼ cup shortening
3 cups powdered sugar
⅓ cup whipping cream
1 teaspoon salt

1. Preheat oven to 350°F. Grease 24 standard (2½-inch) muffin cups. Prepare cake mix according to package directions. Spoon batter into prepared muffin cups, filling two-thirds full.

2. Bake 20 minutes or until toothpick inserted into centers comes out clean. Cool in pans 10 minutes. Remove to wire racks; cool completely.

3. Beat butter and shortening in large bowl with electric mixer at medium speed until well blended. Add powdered sugar, cream and salt; beat at low speed 1 minute. Beat at medium-high speed 2 minutes or until fluffy.

4. Slice tops off cupcakes. Spread filling over bottoms of cupcakes; replace tops.

Makes 24 cupcakes

Island Brownies

1¼ cups all-purpose flour
⅔ cup unsweetened cocoa powder
1 teaspoon baking powder
1 teaspoon salt
1 teaspoon ground ginger
2 cups sugar
4 eggs, lightly beaten
¾ cup (1½ sticks) butter, melted and cooled
¾ cup chopped macadamia nuts
¼ cup finely chopped crystallized ginger

1. Preheat oven to 350°F. Coat 13×9-inch baking pan with nonstick cooking spray. Combine flour, cocoa, baking powder, salt and ground ginger in medium bowl.

2. Combine sugar, eggs and butter in large bowl; mix well. Add flour mixture, nuts and crystallized ginger; stir until blended. Spread batter in prepared pan.

3. Bake 25 to 30 minutes or until toothpick inserted into center comes out clean. Cool completely in pan on wire rack. *Makes 36 brownies*

Easy Fruit Tarts

12 wonton skins
Vegetable cooking spray
2 tablespoons apple jelly or apricot fruit spread
1½ cups sliced or cut-up fruit such as DOLE® Bananas, Strawberries or Red or Green Seedless Grapes
1 cup nonfat or low-fat yogurt, any flavor

PRESS wonton skins into 12 muffin cups sprayed with vegetable cooking spray, allowing corners to stand up over edges of muffin cups.

BAKE at 375°F. 5 minutes or until lightly browned. Carefully remove wonton cups to wire rack; cool.

COOK and stir jelly in small saucepan over low heat until jelly melts.

BRUSH bottoms of cooled wonton cups with melted jelly. Place two fruit slices in each cup; spoon rounded tablespoon of yogurt on top of fruit. Garnish with fruit slice and mint leaves. Serve immediately. *Makes 12 servings*

Strawberry Angel Food Cake Roll

1 package (16 ounces) angel food cake mix
1¼ cups water
1 cup plus 2 tablespoons powdered sugar, divided
1 package (8 ounces) cream cheese, softened
1½ cups strawberry jam, divided
2 teaspoons vanilla
Additional powdered sugar (optional)
Strawberries (optional)

1. Preheat oven to 350°F. Line 15×10×1-inch jelly-roll pan with parchment paper; spray paper with nonstick cooking spray.

2. Combine cake mix and water in large bowl; mix well. Spread batter evenly in prepared jelly-roll pan; smooth top. Bake 17 to 22 minutes or until light golden brown.

3. Dust top of cake with 2 tablespoons powdered sugar; place clean kitchen towel over top. Invert cake onto towel; peel off parchment paper. Roll cake up with towel from short end. Cool completely on wire rack.

4. Meanwhile, beat cream cheese, remaining 1 cup powdered sugar, ¼ cup jam and vanilla in medium bowl with electric mixer at medium speed until smooth.

5. Unroll cooled cake. Spread cream cheese mixture over cake, leaving 1-inch border. Spread 1 cup jam over cream cheese mixture. Roll up cake.

6. Microwave remaining ¼ cup jam in small microwavable bowl on HIGH 10 seconds; drizzle over top of cake. Dust with additional powdered sugar and garnish with strawberries. *Makes 10 servings*

Milano® Cookie Caramel Ice Cream Cake

1 package (6 ounces) PEPPERIDGE FARM® Milano® Cookies
3 cups vanilla or chocolate ice cream, softened
⅓ cup prepared caramel topping

1. Line an 8-inch round cake pan with plastic wrap.

2. Cut the cookies in half crosswise and arrange around the edge of the pan. Place the remaining cookies into the bottom of the pan.

3. Spread 1½ **cups** ice cream over the cookies. Drizzle with the caramel topping. Spread the remaining ice cream over the caramel topping. Cover and freeze for 6 hours or until the ice cream is firm.

4. Uncover the pan and invert the cake onto a serving plate. Serve with additional caramel topping. *Makes 8 servings*

Kitchen Tip: Substitute chocolate topping for the caramel topping.

Prep Time: 20 minutes • Freeze Time: 6 hours

Chocolate Cinnamon Cake

1 package (about 18 ounces) devil's food cake mix
1¼ cups water
3 eggs
⅓ cup canola oil
1 tablespoon instant coffee granules
1½ to 2 teaspoons ground cinnamon
¼ cup powdered sugar

1. Preheat oven to 350°F. Coat 13×9-inch baking pan with nonstick cooking spray; set aside.

2. Combine cake mix, water, eggs, oil, coffee granules and cinnamon in large bowl. Mix according to package directions. Pour into prepared pan.

3. Bake 25 to 27 minutes or until toothpick inserted into center comes out clean. Cool completely on wire rack. Sift powdered sugar over cake just before serving. *Makes 18 to 20 servings*

Milano® Cookie Caramel Ice Cream Cake

Grape Soda Cupcakes

1½ cups all-purpose flour
1 (0.14-ounce) envelope grape unsweetened drink mix
2 teaspoons baking powder
⅛ teaspoon salt
1 cup granulated sugar
1 cup (2 sticks) unsalted butter, softened, divided
2 eggs
½ cup plus 3 tablespoons milk, divided
1½ teaspoons vanilla, divided
3 cups powdered sugar
Purple gel food coloring
Pearl decors (optional)

1. Preheat oven to 350°F. Line 12 standard (2½-inch) muffin cups with paper baking cups.

2. Whisk flour, drink mix, baking powder and salt in small bowl. Beat granulated sugar and ½ cup (1 stick) butter in medium bowl with electric mixer at medium speed until creamy. Add eggs, one at a time, beating well after each addition. Add flour mixture; beat until blended. Add ½ cup milk and 1 teaspoon vanilla; beat until smooth.

3. Spoon batter evenly into prepared muffin cups. Bake 20 minutes or until toothpick inserted into centers comes out clean. Cool in pan 10 minutes. Remove to wire rack; cool completely.

4. Meanwhile, beat powdered sugar, remaining ½ cup (1 stick) butter, 3 tablespoons milk and ½ teaspoon vanilla in large bowl at medium speed until fluffy. Tint with food coloring. Pipe or spread onto cupcakes. Top with decors, if desired.

Makes 12 cupcakes

Sour Cream Chocolate Cake

- ½ cup HERSHEY'S® Cocoa
- ½ cup hot water
- ½ cup (1 stick) butter or margarine, softened
- 1 cup granulated sugar
- ½ cup packed light brown sugar
- 1½ teaspoons vanilla extract
- 3 eggs
- 1¾ cups all-purpose flour
- 1½ teaspoons baking powder
- 1 teaspoon baking soda
- 1 teaspoon salt
- 1 cup (8 ounces) dairy sour cream
- Quick Fudge Frosting (recipe follows)

1. Heat oven to 350°F. Grease and flour two 9-inch round baking pans.

2. Combine cocoa and water in small bowl; stir until smooth. Set aside.

3. Beat butter in large bowl until creamy. Add granulated sugar, brown sugar and vanilla; beat until fluffy. Add eggs; beat well. Stir in cocoa mixture. Stir together flour, baking powder, baking soda and salt; add alternately with sour cream to butter mixture, beating just until blended. Pour batter into prepared pans.

4. Bake 30 to 35 minutes or until wooden pick inserted in center comes out clean. Cool 15 minutes; remove from pans to wire racks. Cool completely. Frost with Quick Fudge Frosting. *Makes 8 to 10 servings*

Quick Fudge Frosting

- 6 to 7 tablespoons light cream or evaporated milk
- ⅓ cup butter or margarine, softened
- 3 cups powdered sugar
- 6 tablespoons HERSHEY'S® Cocoa
- ⅛ teaspoon salt
- 1 teaspoon vanilla extract

1. Heat cream in small saucepan until bubbles form around edge of pan; remove from heat and set aside.

2. Beat butter in medium bowl until creamy. Stir together powdered sugar, cocoa and salt; add alternately with cream to butter, beating to spreading consistency. Stir in vanilla. *Makes about 2 cups frosting*

Plum Cake with Streusel Topping

Streusel Topping (recipe follows)
1 cup plus 2 tablespoons all-purpose flour
½ teaspoon baking powder
¼ teaspoon salt
¼ teaspoon baking soda
6 tablespoons unsalted butter, softened
¼ cup granulated sugar
¼ cup packed brown sugar
1 teaspoon vanilla
2 eggs
¼ cup buttermilk
3 medium plums, pitted and cut into 8 wedges*

**Plums should be underripe but slightly soft to the touch.*

1. Preheat oven to 350°F. Grease 9-inch springform pan. Line bottom of pan with parchment paper; grease paper. Prepare Streusel Topping.

2. Combine flour, baking powder, salt and baking soda in medium bowl.

3. Beat butter in large bowl with electric mixer at medium speed 1 minute. Add sugars; beat 1 minute or until light and fluffy. Beat in vanilla. Add eggs, one at a time, beating well after each addition.

4. Add flour mixture alternately with buttermilk, beating well on low speed after each addition. Spread batter in prepared pan.

5. Arrange plum wedges around outer edge of batter and in center. Sprinkle with Streusel Topping. Bake 30 minutes or until cake springs back when lightly touched.

6. Place cake on cooling rack. Loosen side of pan and remove. Cool 20 minutes. Serve warm or at room temperature. *Makes 6 servings*

Streusel Topping: Combine ¼ cup all-purpose flour, 3 tablespoons packed brown sugar and ½ teaspoon ground cinnamon in medium bowl. Mix in 2 tablespoons softened unsalted butter with fingers until flour mixture is crumbly.

Dark Chocolate Coconut Cake

- 1 package (about 18 ounces) devil's food cake mix, plus ingredients to prepare mix
- 1 cup strong coffee
- ½ cup evaporated milk
- 4 tablespoons butter, divided
- 3 cups mini marshmallows*
- 1 package (14 ounces) shredded coconut
- 1 cup whipping cream
- 2 cups (12 ounces) semisweet chocolate chips**

**Or substitute 24 large marshmallows.*
***For more intense chocolate flavor, use bittersweet or dark chocolate chips.*

1. Preheat oven to 350°F. Coat two 8-inch cake pans with nonstick cooking spray. Prepare cake mix according to package directions, substituting coffee for water. Divide batter between prepared pans. Bake 23 to 25 minutes or until toothpick inserted into centers comes out clean. Cool completely in pans on wire rack.

2. For filling, bring evaporated milk and 2 tablespoons butter to a boil in medium saucepan over medium heat. Add marshmallows; stir until smooth. Stir in coconut. Cool completely.

3. For topping, heat cream and remaining 2 tablespoons butter in medium saucepan over medium-low heat until just hot. (Do not boil.) Remove from heat; add chocolate chips. Let stand 1 minute; stir until smooth. Keep warm.

4. Cut each cake layer in half horizontally. Place one layer on serving plate; spread with one third of filling almost to edge. Repeat with remaining cake layers and filling. Spread topping over assembled cake. Chill to firm topping before serving. Store leftovers in refrigerator. *Makes 12 to 16 servings*

Slow Cooker Sticky Caramel Pumpkin Cake

2 cups all-purpose flour
2 teaspoons baking powder
1 teaspoon baking soda
½ teaspoon salt
½ teaspoon pumpkin pie spice or ground cinnamon
1⅓ cups sugar
1 cup (2 sticks) unsalted butter, at room temperature
4 eggs, at room temperature
1 can (15 ounces) solid-pack pumpkin
1 jar (16 ounces) caramel sauce or caramel ice cream topping

Slow Cooker Directions

1. Coat 4½-quart slow cooker with nonstick cooking spray.

2. Whisk flour, baking powder, baking soda, salt and pumpkin pie spice in large bowl. Beat sugar and butter in another large bowl with electric mixer at high speed 3 minutes or until light. Add eggs, one at a time, beating well after each addition. Beat in pumpkin. Gradually add flour mixture and beat at low speed until smooth. Spread evenly in slow cooker.

3. Cover; cook on HIGH 2 to 2½ hours or until toothpick inserted into center comes out clean. Drizzle ½ cup caramel sauce over cake. Spoon cake into serving dishes. Serve with additional caramel sauce.

Makes 8 servings

Serving Suggestion: For a fancier presentation, trim a sheet of parchment paper to fit the bottom of the stoneware insert. Spray the insert with nonstick cooking spray, then line with trimmed parchment paper and spray again. Proceed as above but before drizzling with caramel sauce, place a plate upside-down on top of the stoneware and invert cake onto plate. Peel parchment paper from bottom of cake, then invert onto serving plate.

Apricot Nectar Cake

4 cups all-purpose flour, plus additional for dusting pan
1 teaspoon baking powder
¾ teaspoon baking soda
¾ teaspoon salt
1 cup (2 sticks) unsalted butter, softened
2½ cups sugar, divided
4 eggs
2 cups apricot nectar, divided
¾ cup buttermilk
Grated peel of 1 lemon
Juice of 1 lemon
Powdered sugar

1. Preheat oven to 325°F. Grease and flour 10- or 12-cup bundt pan.

2. Combine 4 cups flour, baking powder, baking soda and salt in medium bowl.

3. Beat butter in large bowl with electric mixer at medium speed until smooth. Beat in 2 cups sugar until blended. Add eggs, one at a time, beating well after each addition.

4. Combine 1½ cups nectar and buttermilk in small bowl. Alternately add flour mixture and nectar mixture to butter mixture, beating after each addition. Stir in lemon peel. Pour batter into prepared pan.

5. Bake 1 hour or until cake springs back when lightly touched. Cool in pan 15 minutes.

6. Meanwhile, combine remaining ½ cup sugar, ½ cup nectar and lemon juice in small saucepan. Bring to a boil over medium-low heat. Boil 1 minute; remove from heat.

7. Invert cake onto serving plate. Poke holes in top and sides with wooden skewer. Brush top and sides of cake with syrup, allowing it to soak into cake. Cool completely.

Makes 16 servings

Cannoli Cupcakes

- 2 cups all-purpose flour
- ½ teaspoon baking soda
- ½ teaspoon baking powder
- ½ teaspoon salt
- 1 cup granulated sugar
- ½ cup (1 stick) unsalted butter, softened
- 1 cup whole-milk ricotta cheese
- 1 teaspoon grated orange peel
- 1 egg
- 2 teaspoons vanilla, divided
- 1 cup whipping cream
- 8 ounces mascarpone cheese, softened
- ½ cup powdered sugar
- Mini semisweet chocolate chips and chopped unsalted pistachios (optional)

1. Preheat oven to 350°F. Line 15 standard (2½-inch) muffin cups with paper baking cups.

2. Whisk flour, baking soda, baking powder and salt in small bowl. Beat granulated sugar and butter in large bowl with electric mixer at medium speed until creamy. Add ricotta cheese and orange peel; beat until blended. Add egg and 1 teaspoon vanilla; beat until blended. Spoon batter evenly into prepared muffin cups.

3. Bake 20 minutes or until toothpick inserted into centers comes out clean. Cool in pans 10 minutes. Remove to wire racks; cool completely.

4. Meanwhile, beat cream in medium bowl at high speed until stiff peaks form. Stir together mascarpone cheese, powdered sugar and remaining 1 teaspoon vanilla in another medium bowl. Fold whipped cream into mascarpone mixture until blended. Frost cupcakes. Garnish with chocolate chips and pistachios.

Makes 15 cupcakes

Lemon-Orange Party Cake

1 package (about 18 ounces) yellow cake mix with pudding in the mix
1¼ cups plus 5 tablespoons orange juice, divided
3 eggs
⅓ cup vegetable oil
2 tablespoons grated orange peel
5½ cups sifted powdered sugar, divided
⅓ cup lemon juice
⅓ cup butter, softened
Colored sprinkles
20 candy fruit slices

1. Preheat oven to 350°F. Lightly grease 13×9-inch baking pan.

2. Beat cake mix, 1¼ cups orange juice, eggs, oil and orange peel in large bowl with electric mixer at low speed 1 minute or until blended. Beat at medium speed 1 to 2 minutes or until smooth. Spread in prepared pan.

3. Bake 30 to 35 minutes or until toothpick inserted into center comes out clean. Meanwhile, combine 1 cup powdered sugar and lemon juice in small bowl; stir until smooth.

4. Pierce top of warm cake with wooden skewer at ½-inch intervals. Slowly drizzle lemon glaze over warm cake. Cool completely.

5. Beat remaining 4½ cups powdered sugar and butter in large bowl with electric mixer at low speed until blended. Beat in enough remaining orange juice to reach spreading consistency. Spread frosting over cooled cake. Decorate top of cake with sprinkles and candy fruit slices.

Makes 20 servings

Amazing Red Devil's Food Cake

2½ cups all-purpose flour
½ cup unsweetened cocoa powder
1½ teaspoons baking soda
¼ teaspoon salt
½ cup (1 stick) butter, softened
1¾ cups sugar
2 eggs
1 teaspoon vanilla extract
1½ cups CAMPBELL'S® Tomato Juice
Creamy Butter Frosting (recipe follows)

1. Heat the oven to 350°F. Grease and flour 2 (8-inch) round cake pans.

2. Stir the flour, cocoa, baking soda and salt in a medium bowl.

3. Beat the butter and sugar in a large bowl with an electric mixer on medium speed until the mixture is light and fluffy. Beat in the eggs, one at a time, beating well after each addition. Beat in the vanilla extract.

4. Reduce the speed to low. Add the flour mixture alternately with the tomato juice, beating well after each addition. Pour the batter into the cake pans.

5. Bake for 35 minutes or until a toothpick inserted in the center comes out clean. Cool the cakes in the pans on wire racks for 10 minutes. Remove the cakes from the pans and cool completely on the wire racks. Frost and fill with the Creamy Butter Frosting. Refrigerate until ready to serve.

Makes 12 servings

Creamy Butter Frosting: Place ¾ cup (1½ sticks) butter, softened, 1 package (16 ounces) confectioners' sugar, ¼ cup milk, ½ teaspoon vanilla extract and ¼ teaspoon salt in a medium bowl. Beat with an electric mixer on low speed until the mixture is smooth. Increase the speed to medium, adding more milk, if needed, until desired consistency. Makes 2½ cups.

Prep Time: 15 minutes • **Bake Time:** 35 minutes • **Cool Time:** 40 minutes

Boston Cream Pie

1 package (3.4 ounces) JELL-O® Vanilla Flavor Instant Pudding
1 cup cold milk
1½ cups thawed COOL WHIP® Whipped Topping
1 round yellow cake layer (8- or 9-inch)
1 square BAKER'S® Unsweetened Chocolate
1 tablespoon butter
¾ cup powdered sugar
2 tablespoons cold milk

1. BEAT pudding mix and 1 cup milk with whisk 2 minutes. Stir in COOL WHIP®. Let stand 5 minutes. Meanwhile, cut cake horizontally into 2 layers with serrated knife.

2. STACK cake layers on serving plate, spreading pudding mixture between layers.

3. MICROWAVE chocolate and butter in medium microwavable bowl on HIGH 1 minute; stir until chocolate is melted. Add sugar and 2 tablespoons milk; mix well. Spread over cake. Refrigerate 1 hour.

Makes 10 servings

Tip: To slice cooled cake layers evenly, place on serving plate. Make a 2-inch horizontal cut around side of cake using a long serrated knife. Then, cut all of the way through the cake layer to make 2 layers.

Prep Time: 15 minutes plus refrigerating

Mini Oreo® Surprise Cupcakes

1 package (2-layer size) chocolate cake mix
1 package (8 ounces) PHILADELPHIA® Cream Cheese, softened
1 egg
2 tablespoons sugar
48 Mini OREO® Bite Size Chocolate Sandwich Cookies
1½ cups thawed COOL WHIP® Whipped Topping

1. PREHEAT oven to 350°F. Prepare cake batter as directed on package; set aside. Beat cream cheese, egg and sugar until well blended.

2. SPOON cake batter into 24 paper- or foil-lined 2½-inch muffin cups, filling each cup about half full. Top each with about 1½ teaspoons of the cream cheese mixture and 1 cookie. Cover evenly with remaining cake batter.

3. BAKE 19 to 22 minutes or until wooden toothpick inserted in centers comes out clean. Cool 5 minutes; remove from pans to wire racks. Cool completely. (There may be an indentation in top of each cupcake after baking.) Top cupcakes with whipped topping and remaining cookies just before serving. Store in tightly covered container in refrigerator up to 3 days.

Makes 24 cupcakes

Make it Easy: For easy portioning of cream cheese mixture into cake batter, spoon cream cheese mixture into large resealable plastic bag. Seal bag securely. Snip small corner of bag with scissors. Squeeze about 1½ teaspoons of the cream cheese mixture over batter in each muffin cup.

Prep Time: 10 minutes • Bake Time: 22 minutes

OREO

Zucchini Spice Bundt Cake

1 package (about 18 ounces) spice or carrot cake mix
1 cup water
3 eggs
2 tablespoons canola oil
1 medium zucchini, shredded
3 tablespoons chopped walnuts, toasted*
¾ teaspoon vanilla
¼ cup powdered sugar
1 to 2 teaspoons milk

**To toast walnuts, spread in single layer on baking sheet. Bake in preheated 325°F oven 7 to 10 minutes or until golden brown, stirring frequently.*

1. Preheat oven to 325°F. Spray 12-cup bundt pan with nonstick cooking spray.

2. Combine cake mix, water, eggs and oil in large bowl; mix according to package directions. Stir in zucchini, walnuts and vanilla until well blended. Pour into prepared pan.

3. Bake 40 to 45 minutes or until toothpick inserted near center comes out almost clean. Cool in pan 10 minutes. Invert onto wire rack; cool completely.

4. For glaze, combine powdered sugar and milk in small bowl; stir until smooth. Drizzle glaze evenly over cake. *Makes 18 servings*

The publisher would like to thank the companies and organizations listed below for the use of their recipes and photographs in this publication.

BelGioioso® Cheese Inc.

Campbell Soup Company

Dole Food Company, Inc.

The Hershey Company

Hillshire Farm®

Kraft Foods Global, Inc.

Nestlé USA

Ortega®, A Division of B&G Foods, Inc.

Publications International, Ltd.

Recipes courtesy of the Reynolds Kitchens

Riviana Foods Inc.

Unilever

VOLUME MEASUREMENTS (dry)

1/8 teaspoon = 0.5 mL
1/4 teaspoon = 1 mL
1/2 teaspoon = 2 mL
3/4 teaspoon = 4 mL
1 teaspoon = 5 mL
1 tablespoon = 15 mL
2 tablespoons = 30 mL
1/4 cup = 60 mL
1/3 cup = 75 mL
1/2 cup = 125 mL
2/3 cup = 150 mL
3/4 cup = 175 mL
1 cup = 250 mL
2 cups = 1 pint = 500 mL
3 cups = 750 mL
4 cups = 1 quart = 1 L

VOLUME MEASUREMENTS (fluid)

1 fluid ounce (2 tablespoons) = 30 mL
4 fluid ounces (1/2 cup) = 125 mL
8 fluid ounces (1 cup) = 250 mL
12 fluid ounces (1 1/2 cups) = 375 mL
16 fluid ounces (2 cups) = 500 mL

WEIGHTS (mass)

1/2 ounce = 15 g
1 ounce = 30 g
3 ounces = 90 g
4 ounces = 120 g
8 ounces = 225 g
10 ounces = 285 g
12 ounces = 360 g
16 ounces = 1 pound = 450 g

DIMENSIONS

1/16 inch = 2 mm
1/8 inch = 3 mm
1/4 inch = 6 mm
1/2 inch = 1.5 cm
3/4 inch = 2 cm
1 inch = 2.5 cm

OVEN TEMPERATURES

250°F = 120°C
275°F = 140°C
300°F = 150°C
325°F = 160°C
350°F = 180°C
375°F = 190°C
400°F = 200°C
425°F = 220°C
450°F = 230°C

BAKING PAN SIZES

Utensil	Size in Inches/Quarts	Metric Volume	Size in Centimeters
Baking or Cake Pan (square or rectangular)	8×8×2	2 L	20×20×5
	9×9×2	2.5 L	23×23×5
	12×8×2	3 L	30×20×5
	13×9×2	3.5 L	33×23×5
Loaf Pan	8×4×3	1.5 L	20×10×7
	9×5×3	2 L	23×13×7
Round Layer Cake Pan	8×1½	1.2 L	20×4
	9×1½	1.5 L	23×4
Pie Plate	8×1¼	750 mL	20×3
	9×1¼	1 L	23×3
Baking Dish or Casserole	1 quart	1 L	—
	1½ quart	1.5 L	—
	2 quart	2 L	—